Uncle John's BATHROOM READER® PLUNGES INTO MINNESOTA

Bathroom Readers' Hysterical Society

San Diego, California

The following are registered trademarks: "Bathroom Reader,"
"Bathroom Readers' Institute," "Portable Press," and
"Uncle John's Bathroom Reader."

For information, write the Bathroom Readers' Hysterical Society
Portable Press, 5880 Oberlin Drive, San Diego, CA 92121
e-mail: unclejohn@advmkt.com

ISBN 13: 978-1-59223-380-9
ISBN 10: 1-59223-380-5

Library of Congress Cataloging-in-Publication Data
is available

Printed in the United States of America
First printing: July 2006

06 07 08 09 10   10 9 8 7 6 5 4 3 2 1

Project Team

JoAnn Padgett, Director, Editorial and Production
Melinda Allman, Developmental Editor
Jennifer Payne, Production Editor
Jennifer Thornton, Managing Editor
Connie Vazquez, Product Manager

Thank You!

The Bathroom Readers' Hysterical Society sincerely
thanks the following additional people whose advice
and assistance made this book possible.

Toney Allman	Julia Papps
Michael Brunsfeld	Clare Pavelka
Karen J. Fisher	Barb Porsche
Mary Lou GoForth	Stephen Raymer
Kristine Hemp	Larry Ellis Reed
Gordon Javna	Tamar Schwartz
Keith Kahla	Jennifer Skancke
Eugene Myers	Sydney Stanley
Laurel Nelson	Nancy Toeppler
Kent Nyberg	Lisa Winterhalder
Allen Orso	Thomas Crapper

Hysterical Scholars

The Bathroom Readers' Hysterical Society sincerely
thanks the following talented people who
contributed selections to this work.

Melinda Allman

Joan Brandwein

Myles Callum

Jenness I. Crawford

Jacqueline Damian

Padraic Duffy

Vickey Kalambakal

Robin Kilrain

Andy Levy-Ajzenkopf

Jane Lott

Danielle Markson

Lea Markson

Ryan Murphy

Debbie Pawlak

Jennifer Payne

William Dylan Powell

Betty Sleep

Stephanie Spadaccini

Susan Steiner

Diana Moes VandeHoef

Contents

Good Sports

History

Hometowns

Puzzles

Speaking Minnesotan

Answers

Preface

Welcome to Minnesota!

We're excited to make the North Star State the latest volume in Uncle John's regional Bathroom Reader series because nowhere else is the lutefisk as tender, the winter as wondrous, or the reception as warm. So grab your fishing pole and bring along your best Scandinavian accent. We're taking the plunge into the Land of 10,000 Lakes.

The home of Prince, Keillor, and a big ball of twine. It's the place where Mary Tyler Moore made it after all and Laura Ingalls Wilder lived underground. When it comes to culture, cleverness, and kitsch, Minnesota's got it. So Uncle John recruited a group of Minnesota lovers to put together this collection of the most interesting tales the state has to offer. Here's a sampling:

History: From bringing down bandits to striking with Teamsters to battling the Confederacy at Gettysburg, Minnesotans have played fundamental roles in some of America's most pivotal historical events.

Hometowns: If you want to visit the Hockey Hall of Fame, the birthplace of the Eskimo Pie, or the smallest town in the United States, you can do it in Minnesota.

Business and Industry: Minnesota is the birthplace of many of America's most recognizable brands. Find out the history behind Target, General Mills, Pillsbury, Green Giant, Tonka Toys, and others.

Sports: Whether you're a fan of the Wild, the Vikings, or Carleton College's naked softball games, we've got it covered.

And if you have questions...

- Why are the Twin Cities called "twins"?
- Just how many bathrooms are there inside the Mall of America?
- Where's the world's largest prairie chicken?
- Why did Hall of Famer Dave Winfield swing a sledge-hammer in the on-deck circle?
- How did General Mills' Gold Medal flour get its name?
- Who haunts the Guthrie Theater?
- What's the deal with the Kensington rune stone?

We have answers.

So relax, grab a Spamwich, and join us for this journey through a state that has so much more to offer than ice, wind, freezing temperatures, and snow.

As always, go with the flow . . .

Fact or Fiction?

One of Minnesota's most enduring mysteries involves the Kensington rune stone, an engraved rock that may or may not prove Scandinavians reached the interior of America long before Columbus. The evidence on both sides is compelling. What do you think?

The Story

In 1898, a Swedish immigrant farmer named Olof Ohman and his ten-year-old son Edward found a flat stone slab buried beneath a tree on their property. The Ohmans were clearing the hillside for farming and digging up trees that would be in the way of their field. The gray stone was 30 inches long, 16 inches wide, 6 inches thick, and weighed 200 pounds. It was buried facedown six inches below the surface and was completely tangled in the tree's roots. Edward noticed that the stone was engraved with symbols, but neither he nor his father nor anyone they knew understood what the symbols meant. So Ohman lugged the stone home and, ever the practical Minnesotan, used it as a doorstop in his granary.

Pretty soon, though, word got around about the stone. It went first to the University of Minnesota to be examined and then on to the University of Chicago. Copies of the inscription were even sent to scientists in Norway. The symbols etched into the stone, it turns out, were runes—a type of writing used by ancient Scandinavians—and they conveyed the following message:

Eight Goths and 22 Norwegians on a journey of explo-
ration from Vinland very far west. We had camp by two
rocky islands one day's journey north from this stone. We
were out fishing one day. After we came home we found 10
men red with blood and dead. Ave Maria save us from evil.
Have 10 men by the sea to look after our ships 14 days'
journey from this island. Year 1362.

Year 1362? That was 130 years before Columbus arrived in
the New World and more than 300 years after Viking Leif
Eriksson landed in Newfoundland and called the area Vinland.
Given those facts, the men studying the stone were left with one
main question: Was the stone for real, or was it a hoax perpetu-
ated by Scandinavian immigrants eager to prove that their ancestors, and not the Italians, had actually discovered America?

Most scholars called the stone a forgery, but some believed
it was true. Many laypeople were also convinced of the stone's
authenticity. In 1907, a University of Wisconsin graduate student named Hjalmar Holand bought the stone from Ohman. It's
unclear exactly how much Holand paid, but by all accounts, it
was between $1 and $10. Holand then took the stone to
Minnesota Historical Society geologist Newton Horace
Winchell and linguist George Flom from the University of
Illinois. After careful examination, the men published conflict-
ing opinions in 1910: Winchell deemed the stone authentic,
and Flom called it a fake.

The debate about the stone's authenticity has raged for
the last 100 years. Linguists, runic scholars, and archeologists
all over the world have studied the stone and continue to
disagree.

At one point, the stone was called an absolute forgery, but in the 1940s, it was displayed at the Smithsonian Institute in Washington, D.C., and called one of North America's most important archeological finds. There is still no consensus, so Uncle John has pieced together the evidence for and against and will let you decide.

Evidence of a Hoax

- No one can prove Olof Ohman's story is true. He and his son removed the stone from its resting place, cut down the tree, and plowed the field. There's no way to verify that the stone was found as they claimed.
- The face of the stone doesn't appear to show enough weathering to have spent 500 years in the freezing, thawing, and refreezing Minnesota ground.
- Some of the runes seem to show English words not used in Scandinavia during the 14th century.
- As far as scholars know, the rune for the word *opdagelsefard*, which means "voyage of discovery," wasn't part of the Scandinavian language until several hundred years after the 1362 date on the stone.
- Historical record shows that Scandinavians were sea explorers, not land explorers, so it's unlikely that they would have ventured so far into North America.

Evidence of Authenticity

- Olof Ohman was an uneducated immigrant. He probably would not have had the knowledge of ancient runes needed to create the stone.

- The back of the stone shows more weathering than the face. Since Ohman said he found the stone facedown, it's possible that the face would be less weathered.
- Cormorant Lake, near the spot of the stone's discovery, may have been the place where the explorers camped. Boulders with drilled holes that resemble Norwegian mooring rocks have been found at Cormorant Lake. Ancient Norse explorers used these types of boulders to anchor their boats.
- There was a Scandinavian expedition to Greenland in the 1360s, and some of the explorers ventured beyond that original destination. One of the explorers wrote a book about the expedition, and although no copies of that book exist today, it is referenced in other historical works. This leads scholars to believe the book and the expedition did exist, though they don't know exactly where the explorers went.

That's It?

There is an alternative theory. Perhaps the stone is authentic but was not etched in Minnesota. Some scientists have suggested that it was moved from its original spot on the coast and brought to Minnesota on a later expedition. Who would have carried it and why, however, remain a mystery.

Whether real or fake, the rune stone continues to be the source of great speculation and mystery in Minnesota, and all the debate doesn't appear to be dying down anytime soon. So if you want to get in on the discussion or just examine the rune stone for yourself, take a trip to Alexandria, Minnesota, where it is currently on display at the Runestone Museum.

Minnesota on the Map

Your guide to some of the cities, towns, and
communities discussed in the following pages.

Humboldt

International Falls

Grand Marais

Hibbing
Bovey   Eveleth
Grand Rapids

Duluth

Alexandria   Little Falls   Hinckley
Sauk Centre
Tenney   Freeport

Saint Paul
Minneapolis
Bloomington

Red Wing
Walnut Grove   Wabasha
Northfield
Rochester
Worthington   Blue Earth
Austin

Just the Facts, Ma'am

Take a quick look at Minnesota.

Population: 5,100,958

Capital: Saint Paul

State motto: *L'Etoile du Nord* ("The Star of the North")

Land area: 79,610 square miles

Length (north to south): 411 miles

Width (east to west): 357 miles

Highest point: Eagle Mountain, 2,301 feet

Lowest point: Lake Superior, 602 feet

Total area of inland water: 4,779 square miles

Average January temperature: 11.2 degrees

Average July temperature: 73.1 degrees

Record low temperature: -60 degrees (1996)

Record high temperature: 114 degrees (1917 and 1936)

Average annual precipitation: 28.32 inches

Average annual snowfall: 49.6 inches

Organized as a territory: March 3, 1849

Gained statehood: May 11, 1858 (32nd state to enter the Union)

Number of U.S. Representatives: 8

Voter turnout in the 2004 presidential election: 77.3% (the highest in the United States)

Number of counties: 87

Number of state parks: 66 (226,000 acres)

Number of state forests: 58 (almost 4 million acres)

Number of national parks: 2 (Voyageurs and Isle Royale, shared with Michigan)

Borders: Iowa, North Dakota, South Dakota, Wisconsin, and Canada

Rankings among all 50 states
(source: Morgan Quinto Press, 2005):
Most Livable State: #2
Healthiest State: #4
Smartest State: #7

DID YOU KNOW?

Coniferous forest covers 40 percent of the state of Minnesota.

My Saint's as Good as Yours!

A Finnish patron saint born in Minnesota? Now there's a story!

Winters are long in Minnesota. By the time March 17 (Saint Patrick's Day) rolls around, the locals know spring is in the air and are ready for a rollicking good carouse. And carouse they do. Which got Richard Mattson thinking . . .

He Was Finnish Before He Started

It may have been a bit too much of the green beer that did it on Saint Patrick's Day in 1956. But Richard Mattson, an employee of Ketola's Department Store in Virginia, Minnesota, suddenly found himself consumed with jealousy at all the fun the people of Irish descent were having. Not that he wasn't having a good time himself; he was celebrating along with the best of them. It was just that Mattson, whose ancestors came from Finland, thought his people deserved festivities of their own.

Mattson's plan was simple: invent a Finnish saint to rival Saint Patrick, and declare March 16 his feast day. The date was strategically crucial to the plan. If all went well, there would be two days of celebration to chase away those winter blues instead of just one. That the date would also steal a little thunder from the Irish celebrations didn't hurt a bit. Mattson just needed a hook.

Poisonous . . . Frogs?

If Ireland's saint drove away the island's snake population, Mattson theorized, Finland certainly could have been cleansed of poisonous frogs. Granted, frogs have never been much of a problem in Finland. In fact, frogs don't generally do well in cold climates like Finland's. No matter. Mattson didn't let those pesky details stop him from pushing forward with his plan.

Mattson wasn't the only one who liked the idea of a Finnish saint's day. Many people thought he was on to something. Dr. Sulo Havumaki, a psychology professor at Bemidji State College, thought the idea was great, although he believed the legend could be improved. Havumaki changed the frogs to grasshoppers—they're both jumping critters, after all. And to give the legend a little more drama, Havumaki's story claimed that the grasshoppers were attacking Finland's vineyards.

The details get tricky here. Meticulous readers will no doubt question the veracity of the grasshopper legend, noting that Finland is not generally known for growing grapes and hasn't got much of a wine industry. Picky, picky.

Name That Saint

Now came the important part. What should they name the new "saint"? Mattson and his supporters needed a name with gravitas, a name that sounded, well . . . saintly. It just so happened that Urho Kekkonen became president of Finland that year (1956). Urho is a common Finnish name, and it sounded just right, Mattson decided. Thus, Saint Urho was born. He became the patron saint of Finland and of vineyard workers.

Can You Hear the Music, Grasshopper?

According to the legend, Saint Urho faced down the grasshoppers by shouting in a booming voice, *Heinässirkka, heinässirkka, mene täältä hiiteen.* That strange-looking mouthful means, "Grasshopper, grasshopper, go to hell." And the grasshoppers listened, thereby saving Finland's vineyards and the vintners' jobs. Out of respect, revelers on Saint Urho's Day wear purple and green: purple for the grapes and green for the grasshoppers.

Mattson's legend spread throughout Minnesota and Canada. The celebration even made its way to Finland, where it continues to be observed with gusto. Mojakka, a Finnish fish stew, is traditionally eaten on Saint Urho's Day, accompanied by green or purple beer.

Back in the United States, there are annual Saint Urho's Day celebrations on March 16 all over the Midwest. The most popular take place in the Minnesota towns of Finlayson, Menahga, and Finland, where one of the main events is the crowning of a drag queen called Miss Helmi (Helmi is a popular Finnish girl's name, undoubtedly chosen to highlight the fact that the contestants are all male). Saint Urho's Day has even spread west. The town of Hood River, Oregon, holds an annual festival where, according to one Web site, "The Knights of Saint Urho disrobe and dance the tango with the lovely Iron Maidens to inspiring accordion music."

Fly That Flag

There sure is a lot of symbolism on the Minnesota state flag.

The Background

- The flag's official background is royal blue and represents the many lakes for which the state is known. In fact, Minnesota takes its name from a Dakota word that means "sky-tinted waters."
- The first designer of the flag was Amelia Center, who imagined it to include the state's seal on blue on one side and the seal on white on the reverse. That was difficult to produce, however, so in 1957, the flag was redesigned to have a blue background on both sides.

The Seal

- There are 19 stars surrounding the state seal because Minnesota was the 19th state admitted to the Union after the original 13. The largest star represents Minnesota.
- The original state seal included an image of a Native American fleeing on horseback as a white farmer plowed his field; the farmer's gun and powder horn rest nearby. This implied that settlement was possible only with the removal of the native people. In 1983, the seal was redesigned to show the Indian simply passing the farmer, rather than

fleeing him—an attempt to show a more amiable relation-
ship between the two cultures.

- A wreath of lady's slippers, the state flower, surrounds the
seal, and there are three dates woven into the wreath: 1819,
the year Fort Snelling was established; 1858, the year
Minnesota became a state; and 1893, the year the state legislature adopted the official flag.
- Also woven into the wreath is a red banner that proclaims
Minnesota's motto: *L'Etoile du Nord,* "The Star of the North."

DID YOU KNOW?

Minnesota is the second northernmost state in the nation; only
Alaska is farther north.

Saint Paul:
A Capital City

Though not as populous or world famous as its twin,
Minnesota's capital is a town with 'tude.

Town: Saint Paul
Location: Ramsey County
Founding: 1838
Current population: 287,151
Size: 56.2 square miles (bigger than Minneapolis!)
Median age: 31
County seat: Yes

What's in a Name?

Saint Paul was originally known as "Pig's Eye Landing," for
Pierre "Pig's Eye" Parrant, a tavern owner who made the first
land claim in the area. Thankfully, in 1841, a Roman Catholic
missionary named Lucien Galtier came along and took pity on
the city of swine. He built a log chapel, dedicated it to Saint
Paul, and changed the town's name. Seventeen years later,
when the United States admitted Minnesota to the Union, Saint
Paul (*née* Pig's Eye Landing) became the state capital. Take
that, Minneapolis!

Claims to Fame:

- In spite of its heavenly name, Saint Paul was a haven for Prohibition-era gangsters. During the 1920s and 1930s, notorious noteworthies including John Dillinger, Baby Face Nelson, and the Barker gang set up criminal operations in Saint Paul. They robbed banks, trains, and mail trucks; kidnapped hostages for ransom; and caused general mayhem until they were captured or killed by the FBI.

- Since 1910, Saint Paul has been home to the corporate headquarters of 3M (the Minnesota Mining and Manufacturing Company). From waterproof sandpaper to Scotch tape to Post-it notes, 3M has given the world some of its most recognizable and useful products.

- Writer F. Scott Fitzgerald was born in Saint Paul and spent much of his young life there. He attended the Saint Paul Academy, and his first published work was a detective story for the school's newspaper; he was 13.

- Saint Paul is home to America's only full-time professional chamber orchestra, the Saint Paul Chamber Orchestra.

- Billed as America's oldest winter festival, Saint Paul Winter Carnival brings thousands of visitors to the city every year. It all began in 1885, when a New York reporter called winter in Saint Paul "unfit for human habitation." The Saint Paul Chamber of Commerce took offense and held the first Saint Paul Winter Carnival to celebrate the city and to show the world that Minnesotans happily "habitated" in their capital during the winter months.

To read about Minneapolis, turn to page 30.

Grape Expectations

Minnesota vintners' passion for wine and the efforts of local scientists have created a wine industry in a state more often associated with ice fishing, snowmobiles, and beer.

Tough Grapes Don't Whine

In some ways, Southern Minnesota is well suited to producing wine grapes. After all, the famous French vineyards in Bordeaux grow at a latitude of 45 degrees north, the same as Minneapolis. There's a catch, of course: Bordeaux doesn't have Minnesota's short growing season and those killer winters where temperatures drop to -30 degrees.

This fact didn't stop Minnesota wine lovers who tried to grow wine-producing grapes despite the climate. One of the first was August Schell, who founded the August Schell Brewery in 1860. Schell planted vineyards on his estate to make wine for his family, and he did cultivate a small crop, but it was a challenging process.

Traditional French wine grapes can withstand a low temperature of about -5 degrees. Hybrids (French grapes crossed with American varieties) are hardier, but still can only survive temperatures that reach -20 degrees. Given that Minnesota's winter temperatures can be even colder, these grapevines can't make it through the winter there without special protection.

To keep vineyards alive during the winter, Minnesota growers had to detach grapevines from their trellises in the fall, lay them in trenches, and then cover them with soil or straw. The vines remained covered until the spring thaw when they could be retrellised for another crop. For larger vineyards, this meant burying and resurrecting thousands of vines every year, a job that kept costs high. Even for smaller vineyards, it was still a lot of work. And despite this intensive and expensive winter care, there was no guarantee that the vines would thrive come spring.

The Frontenac

What local vintners needed was a grape that could produce a great drinking wine but withstand sleet, snow, and winters of -30 degrees. In the 1970s, researchers at the University of Minnesota began a project of breeding new grape varieties in an attempt to create a cold-hardy wine grape.

After much research and experimentation, the university researchers shared the fruits of their labor in 1996. They introduced a grape for commercial sale that was hardy to about -35 degrees. They named the grape "Frontenac," for a town in the Mississippi River valley where most of Minnesota's wine grapes are grown.

Frontenac grapes were a huge success. They produced a red wine that connoisseurs said had delicious cherry and blackberry overtones. Best of all, Frontenac vines don't have to be buried in winter. The grape is now the most widely grown red-wine grape in Minnesota and has become a mainstay of regional wineries throughout the upper Midwest and Northeast.

After the Frontenac came two more cold-hardy wine grapes: La Crescent (named for one of Minnesota's Mississippi River towns) and Frontenac Gris. La Crescent makes a white wine with apricot, citrus, and pineapple aromas. Frontenac Gris produces a crisp, flavorful blush wine.

A State of Wine

Thanks to these cold-climate grapes, Minnesota's wine industry is growing. In 1998, there were only four bonded wineries in the state. By 2005, there were 16. Below is a list of the Minnesota wineries that use cold-hardy grapes.

Alexis Bailly in Hastings
Falconer Vineyards Winery in Red Wing
Fieldstone Vineyards in Morgan
Cannon River Winery in Cannon Falls
Morgan Creek Vineyards in New Ulm
Saint Croix Vineyards in Stillwater
Brush Wolf Winery in Alexandria

DID YOU KNOW?

The freezing temperatures that created such a challenge for classic wine growers also enabled Minnesotans to specialize in a different imbibing favorite: ice wine. Ice wine is a dessert wine traditionally made in Austria and Germany; immigrants brought the skill with them to Minnesota. To make ice wine, vintners leave white wine grapes to freeze on the vine. The frozen grapes then must be harvested and pressed before they can thaw.

Minnesota's Most
Famous Shy Person

"It's been a quiet week in Lake Wobegon . . . "

In 1985, Time magazine named Garrison Keillor "Minnesota's
Most Famous Shy Person"—an oxymoron, if ever there were
one. As host of the NPR radio show *A Prairie Home Companion*
and author of more than ten books and numerous articles for
newspapers and magazines, Keillor's public persona is anything
but shy.

The Wonder Years
Garrison Keillor was born Gary Edward Keillor on August 7,
1942, in Anoka, Minnesota. His parents were Plymouth
Brethren, a fundamentalist Christian denomination. They were
strict and didn't allow a television in their home until Gary was
a teenager. But they did allow radio, and young Gary liked listening to music. He also wrote poetry. When Gary was 14, he
took the name "Garrison" as a nom de plume to publish his
poems.

Keillor attended the University of Minnesota intermittently
from 1960 to graduation in 1966. He dropped out in 1962 to
work for a local newspaper but soon returned to school. Even
then, though, his attention stayed mostly on writing (specifically

for the student newspaper and literary magazine), and his GPA hovered around 2.0.

He bumped into the radio business by chance as a college freshman. One story Keillor tells has it that he had a crush on a Danish exchange student, so when he learned that the Danish Royal Ballet was performing, he went to the student radio station and offered to interview all of the dancers, hoping to impress her. True or not, the exchange student became his second wife in 1985. It's much more likely, though, that Keillor took a job announcing on the radio because it was easier than washing dishes and paid just as well.

Master of the Airwaves

Still trying to make it as a writer, Keillor saw radio as a source of steady income. In 1969, he got a job as a classical radio announcer at KSJR, the first station in what became Minnesota Public Radio. Soon he was hosting the morning show, his mellifluous voice shepherding Twin Cities commuters to work. At the same time, he started writing stories for the *New Yorker* magazine. The magazine published his first submission, a 400-word story called "Local Family Keeps Son Happy," an impressive feat for an unknown writer. His experience writing for the *New Yorker* was a good one. Keillor says, "I had a great time there and was well treated."

Home, Sweet Prairie

In 1974, the *New Yorker* assigned Keillor to write an article on "The Grand Ole Opry" radio program. This assignment was a turning point for Keillor. The Opry, with its hodgepodge of country music numbers and folksy comedy sketches, inspired him to create a Saturday afternoon radio variety show. Keillor chose the name for his program from a sign in Moorhead, Minnesota: Prairie Home Cemetery. Keillor thought he had better not include the word "cemetery," though.

A Prairie Home Companion debuted on Minnesota Public Radio on July 6, 1974. The first live broadcast was from the theater at Saint Paul's Macalester College. Garrison Keillor stood on the stage in the 400-seat auditorium and performed for 12 audience members, most of them children. There were more people backstage than that!

The show itself was comedic and corny. Keillor interspersed performances from local folk musicians with comedy sketches. He performed a weekly monologue and related the local news. Since public radio is commercial-free, Keillor wrote and performed fictitious commercial spots for fake goods like Powdermilk Biscuits and Jack's Auto Repair of Lake Wobegon. The show, which recalled the campiness of old-time radio, hit just the right nostalgic note.

Lake Wobegon

The centerpiece of *A Prairie Home Companion* and subject of many of Keillor's books is Lake Wobegon (likely a play on the word "woebegone"), Keillor's fictional hometown. Lake Wobegon is based loosely on the small town of Freeport, Minnesota. Keillor says it started out as a way to talk about his friends and family while maintaining a little distance. Over the years, the lives of the Wobegonians, related every week in a 20-minute monologue, have far outstripped their real-world templates.

Lake Wobegon's fame has spread far beyond "the little town that time forgot and decades cannot improve." In fact, many people believe the town to be real—or want it to be. Lake Wobegon was almost included on the American Automobile Association's maps of Minnesota in the 1980s. And NASA astronauts on the space shuttle *Columbia* jokingly sent Keillor an aerial photo of Minnesota with the comment, "Unfortunately, Lake Wobegon is just off the picture."

Fame and Fortune

Keillor continued to do *A Prairie Home Companion* live when it went national in May 1980 because, he believed, a live show was an authentic show. The pauses, mistakes, and mishaps were part of the down-home feel. During one 1986 show, Keillor got so wrapped up in his monologue that he forgot to leave time for the closing credits. As he harangued, a stage-hand walked on and handed him a slip of paper that read, "Three minutes to end of show," then one that read, "90 seconds." Last, he handed Keillor a note that read, "Say good night." Keillor finally signed off.

As the radio show gained listeners, Garrison Keillor's fame boomed. Soon he found reporters camping out in front of his Saint Paul home. This may have been too much. On Valentine's Day in 1987, Keillor announced that he was ending *A Prairie Home Companion*. He held the farewell broadcast to sold-out crowds in June. But you can't keep a Minnesotan quiet for long. In 1988, he returned for his Second Annual Farewell Tour. This was followed by the Third and Fourth Annual Farewell Tours in 1989 and 1990.

Slow and Steady Wins the Race

Keillor traveled and wrote books, but he managed to stay away from radio only for a little while. In the late 1980s, he moved to New York City and, in 1989, started broadcasting *The American Radio Company of the Air* from the Brooklyn Academy of Music. The show closely resembled *A Prairie Home Companion*, though it lacked the Norwegian bachelor farmer jokes. After four years, Keillor's radio show returned to Minnesota and resumed its old name. You can take the boy out of Minnesota, it seems, but you can't take Minnesota out of the boy.

A Prairie Home Companion has been on the air for 30 years—that's more than 3,000 hours of programming. Four million people listen to it every week on 558 stations. And that's not including those who listen over the World Wide Web. What started out as a nostalgic look at Garrison Keillor's rural Minnesota roots has made Lake Wobegon the symbol for Midwestern America. It's easy to see why. After all, Lake Wobegon is, as Keillor says in his monologue each week, a place "where the women are strong, the men are good-looking, and all of the children are above average."

DID YOU KNOW?

In 2006, director Robert Altman released a movie version of *A Prairie Home Companion*, starring Woody Harrelson, Tommy Lee Jones, Meryl Streep, Lindsay Lohan, and Garrison Keillor as himself. Much of the film was shot in and around the Fitzgerald Theater in Saint Paul.

Born in Minnesota

Minnesota has given birth to some of America's most famous artists, athletes, professionals, and politicians. Here's a list of the state's native sons and daughters and the towns from which they came.

Athletes

Jeanne Arth (tennis player, Saint Paul)

Troy Bell (basketball player, Minneapolis)

Charles Bender (baseball player, Brainerd)

Patty Berg (founding member of the Ladies Professional Golf Association, Minneapolis)

Neal Broten (hockey player, Roseau)

Phil Housley (hockey player, Saint Paul)

Kent Hrbek (baseball player, Minneapolis)

Tom Lehman (golfer, Austin)

John Madden (football coach and announcer, Austin)

Roger Maris (baseball player, Hibbing)

Kevin McHale (basketball player, Hibbing)

Paul Molitor (baseball player, Saint Paul)

Jack Morris (baseball player, Saint Paul)

Cindy Nelson (bronze medal winner, Olympic skier, Lutsen)

Dave Winfield (baseball player, Saint Paul)

Performers

Loni Anderson (actress, Saint Paul)

Louie Anderson (comedian, Minneapolis)

Richard Dean Anderson (actor, Minneapolis)

LaVerne Andrews (singer, Minneapolis)

Maxene Andrews (singer, Minneapolis)

Patti Andrews (singer, Minneapolis)

James Arness (actor, Minneapolis)

Tammy Faye Bakker (Christian singer and TV personality, International Falls)

Jessica Biel (actress, Ely)

Rachel Leigh Cook (actress, Minneapolis)

William Demarest (actor, Saint Paul)

Bob Dylan (musician, Duluth)

Kimberly Elise (actress, Minneapolis)

Mike Farrell (actor, Saint Paul)

Judy Garland (actress, Grand Rapids)

Tippi Hedren (actress, New Ulm)

Linda Kelsey (actress, Minneapolis)

Peter Krause (actor, Alexandria)

Jessica Lange (actress, Cloquet)

E. G. Marshall (actor, Owatonna)

Gena Lee Nolin (actress, Duluth)

Prince (musician, Minneapolis)

Marion Ross (actress, Albert Lea)

Jane Russell (actress, Bemidji)

Winona Ryder (actress, Winona)

Sean William Scott (actor, Cottage Grove)

Kevin Sorbo (actor, Mound)

Lea Thompson (actress, Rochester)
Cheryl Tiegs (fashion model, Breckenridge)
Vince Vaughn (actor, Minneapolis)
Gig Young (actor, Saint Cloud)
Steve Zahn (actor, Marshall)

Professionals

Earl Bakken (developed the first wearable pacemaker,
    Minneapolis)
Ann Bancroft (first known woman to reach both the north and
    south poles, Mendota Heights)
Aaron Brown (newscaster, Hopkins)
J. Paul Getty (businessman, Minneapolis)
C. Walton Lillehei (called the "father of modern-day open-
    heart surgery," Minneapolis)
Frank Mars (candy maker, Newport)
Charles Horace Mayo (cofounder of the Mayo Clinic,
    Rochester)
William James Mayo (cofounder of the Mayo Clinic, Le Sueur)
Richard W. Sears (cofounder of Sears, Roebuck and Company,
    Stewartville)
Will Steger (Arctic explorer, Richfield)
Michael Todd (film producer, Minneapolis)
DeWitt Wallace (magazine publisher, cofounded *Reader's
    Digest*, Saint Paul)

Government Officials

Warren E. Burger (former Supreme Court chief justice, Saint
    Paul)

Pierce Butler (former Supreme Court justice, Pine Bend)
William O. Douglas (former Supreme Court justice, Maine)
Eugene McCarthy (politician, Watkins)
Walter Mondale (politician, Ceylon)
Harold Stassen (politician, West Saint Paul)
Jesse Ventura (politician and wrestler, Minneapolis)

Writers and Artists
Carol Bly (author, Duluth)
Robert Bly (author, Madison)
Ethan Coen (screenwriter and filmmaker, Minneapolis)
Joel Coen (screenwriter and filmmaker, Saint Louis Park)
F. Scott Fitzgerald (author, Saint Paul)
Wanda Gag (author and illustrator, New Ulm)
Terry Gilliam (screenwriter, Medicine Lake)
Jon Hassler (author, Minneapolis)
Bill Holm (poet, Minneota)
Jerry Juhl (screenwriter, Saint Paul)
Garrison Keillor (humorist, Anoka)
Sinclair Lewis (author, Sauk Centre)
Maud Hart Lovelace (author, Mankato)
Kate Millet (feminist author, Saint Paul)
LeRoy Neiman (artist, Saint Paul)
Gary Paulsen (author, Minneapolis)
Robert Pirsig (author, Minneapolis)
Charles Schulz (cartoonist, Minneapolis)
Anne Tyler (author, Minneapolis)
Brenda Ueland (author, Minneapolis)

Minnesotans' Thoughts On . . .

Weather

"Behind every gray cloud is another gray cloud."

—*Judy Garland, actress, born in Grand Rapids*

"Winter is not a season, it's an occupation."

—*Sinclair Lewis, author, born in Sauk Centre*

"Some people feel the rain. Others just get wet."

—*Bob Dylan, musician, born in Duluth*

Business

"The meek shall inherit the Earth, but not its mineral rights."

—*J. Paul Getty, businessman, born in Minneapolis*

"Advertising is a valuable economic factor because it is the cheapest way of selling goods, especially if the goods are worthless."

—*Sinclair Lewis*

"I've never been poor, only broke. Being poor is a frame of mind. Being broke is only a temporary situation."

—*Michael Todd, film producer, born in Minneapolis*

Philosophy

"The test of a first-rate intelligence is the ability to hold two opposed ideas in the mind at the same time, and still retain the ability to function."

—F. Scott Fitzgerald, author, born in Saint Paul

"Our American professors like their literature clear, cold, pure and very dead."

—Sinclair Lewis

"I consider myself a poet first and a musician second. I live like a poet and I'll die like a poet."

—Bob Dylan

"There's a difference between a philosophy and a bumper sticker."

—Charles Schulz, cartoonist, born in Minneapolis

Politics

"It is dangerous for a national candidate to say things that people might remember."

"Being in politics is like being a football coach. You have to be smart enough to understand the game, and dumb enough to think it's important."

—Eugene McCarthy, former senator from Minnesota, born in Watkins

Law

"It is not unprofessional to give free legal advice, but advertising that the first visit will be free is a bit like a fox telling chickens he will not bite them until they cross the threshold of the hen house."

—Warren Burger, former chief justice
of the U.S. Supreme Court, born in Saint Paul

"Common sense often makes good law."

"Free speech is not to be regulated like diseased cattle and impure butter. The audience that hissed yesterday may applaud today, even for the same performance."

—William O. Douglas, former justice
of the U.S. Supreme Court, born in Maine

DID YOU KNOW?

Theodore Roosevelt first uttered his famous adage "speak softly and carry a big stick" during a speech at the 1901 Minnesota State Fair.

A Tale of Twin Cities

Hey . . . a little sibling rivalry never hurt anyone.

Town: Minneapolis
Location: Hennepin County
Founding: 1849
Current population: 382,618
Size: 58.4 square miles
Median age: 31.2 years
County seat: Yes

What's in a Name?

The name Minneapolis comes from the Native American word *mine*, which means "water," and the Greek word *polis*, meaning "city." Situated on a plain near the confluence of the Mississippi and Minnesota Rivers and near Saint Anthony Falls, Minneapolis is definitely a "water city."

Claims to Fame:

- Minneapolis is Minnesota's most populous city.
- One of the first Europeans to visit Minneapolis was Father Louis Hennepin in 1680. He was also the one to name the falls after Saint Anthony, the Catholic patron saint of the poor. Before Hennepin, though, the Native Americans had

their own names for the waterfall. The Dakota called it *Minirara*, meaning "curling water," and the Ojibwa called it *Kakabikah*, or "the severed rock."

- In the years before the Civil War, Minneapolis was a premier tourist destination for wealthy travelers from the southern and eastern United States. Most came to see Saint Anthony Falls (sometimes called the Niagara of the West). The onset of the Civil War in 1861 ended the city's run as a major tourist attraction, however, and stunted the city's growth for a time.

- After the Civil War, Minneapolis became known for two things: sawmills and flour mills. By 1880, flour mills dominated, and Minneapolis was the country's top flour producer. The city also gained a reputation for producing the best-quality flour money could buy. From 1880 to 1930, Minneapolis was known as the "Flour Milling Capital of the World."

- The first skyway went up in Minneapolis in 1962. Today, the city has about seven miles of skyways, the most in the United States (Saint Paul has a mere five). More than 260,000 people walk through Minneapolis skyways every day.

- Today, Minneapolis has a thriving arts and theater community. More than 57 museums call Minneapolis home, and the city has more theater seats per capita than any city besides New York.

- Minneapolis is home to 22 of Minnesota's 10,000-plus lakes.

To read about Saint Paul, turn to page 13.

The Mayo Clinic, Part I

*In a business that's famous for professional jealousy,
the Mayo brothers held on to their integrity and their commitment
to sharing knowledge, and created a medical cooperative that
is still considered one of the finest of its kind.*

Before there were the Mayo brothers, there were the Mayo parents, William and Louise. The senior Mayos met in the 1850s, married, and moved to Le Sueur in Minnesota Territory in 1861, the year their oldest son, William, was born. When Will was two years old, the family moved to Rochester. The younger Mayo brother, Charlie, was born there in 1865.

Frontier Medicine

The elder Dr. Mayo was the county coroner as well as a general practitioner. Young Will attended his first postmortem when he was still a toddler. He was so small, in fact, that he had to sit on the examining table to see what his father was doing.
Dr. Mayo's practice was typical of the mid-to-late 1800s. Most of it consisted of assisting at childbirth and treating common ailments like indigestion, measles, or pneumonia. He performed some surgery too, mostly amputations of previously broken limbs that had become infected.

Where There's a Will

Will and Charlie were homeschooled. Mom taught them astronomy and botany, and Dad taught them medical sciences like pathology and anatomy. The boys helped out around their father's office too—rolling bandages and making poultices and salves. When they got a little older, they assisted with operations and prepared microscope slides.

Soon, though, it came time for them to go to medical school. Will went to the University of Michigan, where he was light-years ahead of his classmates. Charlie went to Chicago Medical College (now Northwestern University Medical School), and after graduation in 1888, he set off for Europe.

The Germs of an Idea

While there, Charlie learned of Louis Pasteur's findings about bacteria and how germs caused sickness and infection. This was at a time when only half of the surgeries in the world, mostly in Europe, were performed using the methods of Joseph Lister, the Scottish surgeon who used Pasteur's discoveries to pioneer the idea of antisepsis.

In the interim, big brother Will, now called "Dr. Will" by almost everyone who knew him, had been perfecting his surgical skills. He was performing eye surgery and appendectomies, cutting-edge procedures in the late 1880s. And by the time he was 30, Will had performed more than 100 gallbladder operations, quite an accomplishment given his era and age.

Nuns in the Dance Hall

Charlie returned from Europe to see the Mayos' practice

thriving and their first hospital near completion. William Mayo Senior and a local order of nuns, the Sisters of Saint Francis, had started thinking about the hospital in 1883 when a tornado touched down near Rochester. The town didn't have a hospital to care for all the injured, so Dr. Mayo had to use a local dance hall to house his patients.

After the last tornado victims went home, Mother Alfred, the mother superior at Saint Francis, approached Dr. Mayo and asked him to help her set up a hospital for the city of Rochester. Mother Alfred assured Dr. Mayo that she and her sisters would raise all the necessary money and would serve as the facility's nurses. But the doctor still had misgivings. The strongest was the appalling reputation of 19th century hospitals. Except for a few "modern" facilities on the East Coast, hospitals were charity institutions that served the poor. They were grim and filthy and the perfect place to go if you were ready to die.

Despite Dr. Mayo's hesitation, Mother Alfred and her sisters accumulated enough money over the next four years to build the facility. Faced with all that determination, Dr. Mayo couldn't refuse.

Thank Mother Alfred

The hospital they built together was called Saint Mary's. It was a brick building three stories high and big enough to house 45 patients. Eventually, there would be gaslight fixtures and running water, but at first, the nuns worked by lantern light at night and carried water in buckets from a reservoir in the basement. There was so little money for supplies that the sisters gave up their cots to patients.

Charlie and Will were both on board, and Dr. Mayo invited the local doctors to share in this new venture. They all turned him down. The Protestant doctors didn't want to associate themselves with a Catholic hospital. So the Mayos went it alone at first. After a few years, they assembled a group of talented physicians and technicians to join them.

The hospital charged what a patient could afford, and if a patient couldn't afford the dollar a day for a bed, he wasn't charged. By the end of 1889, its first year in operation, Saint Mary's had seen 62 patients; the next year 300 more; and in 1893, the number reached 1,000.

Clean Living

At first, Dr. Mayo watched with a skeptical eye as his sons applied Lister's antiseptic method, washing and spraying everything with carbolic acid. The senior Mayo soon realized that Lister's method had revolutionized surgery: Doctors could now operate inside the body without fearing infection.

Dr. Will and Dr. Charlie continued learning new techniques. They traveled to large American cities to observe the work of other surgeons who also subscribed to Lister's method. At Johns Hopkins in Baltimore they learned to sterilize their equipment by boiling it in water rather than spraying everything with antiseptics, and to use gowns, masks, and thin rubber gloves to keep themselves and their patients germ-free.

Special Treatment

The Mayo brothers were diagnostic wizards for their time and seemed to be able to identify illnesses (from the simple to the complex) that others could not. Will, for instance, was one of the first doctors in Minnesota who easily recognized something as simple as appendicitis. And on seeing a five-year-old boy who couldn't walk or talk, and who had the stature and gait of a mentally handicapped child, Dr. Charlie diagnosed and treated him for thyroid deficiency. The boy recovered.

Out-of-Towners

The brothers remained virtually unknown outside Minnesota until 1896, when Will read his first paper at the annual meeting of the American Medical Association. There were some disbelievers. But one by one, even they were convinced. Some traveled to Rochester to investigate. What they found amazed them: Waiting rooms overflowed with patients and the surgical skill of the Mayo doctors was breathtaking. All left Saint Mary's impressed by Will and Charlie.

Soon surgeons from around the world were traveling to Rochester to watch the Mayos at work. The brothers rigged a couple of platforms in the operating room so the other doctors could watch without obstruction. The Mayos talked about the patient's history and the diagnosis while they operated, pointing out the finer details of each procedure. Doctors across America started referring their own patients to the Mayos, and some doctors even became Mayo patients themselves.

For the rest of the Mayo story, turn to page 173.

Vikings by the Numbers

Since joining the NFL in 1961, the Minnesota Vikings have been a formidable team. The Purple People Eaters have won 16 division championships and made four trips to the Super Bowl.

0

Number of times the Vikings have won the Super Bowl

2

Vikings who have won the NFL's Most Valuable Player award (Alan Page, 1971; Fran Tarkenton, 1975)

4

Draft choices the Vikings received in return for quarterback Fran Tarkenton on March 7, 1967. Those picks were used to select Clinton Jones, Bob Grim, Ron Yary, and Ed White.

5

Players (including two first-round draft choices) the Vikings traded in 1972 in order to reacquire Tarkenton. The players were Norm Snead, Bob Grim, and Vince Clements

6

Jersey numbers retired by the Vikings (#10 Fran Tarkenton,

#53 Mick Tingelhoff, #70 Jim Marshall, #77 Korey Stringer, #80 Cris Carter, #88 Alan Page)

8

Vikings enshrined in the Pro Football Hall of Fame (Carl Eller, Jim Finks, Bud Grant, Paul Krause, Warren Moon, Alan Page, Fran Tarkenton, and Ron Yary); and consecutive 1,000-yard seasons recorded by wide receiver Cris Carter (1993–2000)

11

Division titles the Vikings achieved under coach Bud Grant during his 18 seasons with the team

17

Touchdown receptions by wide receiver Randy Moss during his 1998 rookie season

556

Points the Vikings scored during their 1998 season. The team went 15–1 that year, and the score set an NFL record.

$10,000

Fine wide receiver Randy Moss received for pretending to moon a crowd of Packers fans after a January 2005 touchdown reception

63,995

Average home attendance in 2005

School Daze: Traditions

Minnesota colleges are known for turning out first-rate scholars who also know how to enjoy themselves. Here are some of the fun traditions Minnesota college students participate in when they're not in the classroom.

Carleton College

Carleton may be small (it's home to only about 1,900 students), but the college offers at least three unique traditions to keep Carletonians' spirits high and senses of humor honed during their stay at the school.

Naked Softball

One favorite is an annual softball game. Begun in 1964, the game was originally part of the school's intramural softball league. Today any student can participate. In this game, there are as many innings as the number of years the school has been open; Carleton was founded in 1866, so in 2006, they were up to 140 innings. All those innings mean the games last for hours, sometimes days. To keep up their stamina, players and spectators fortify themselves with large quantities of beer. And when enthusiasm starts to wane (after maybe a hundred innings or so), the teams play an entirely naked inning or two in an effort to revive the crowd. It usually works.

Cook Me a Cookie

Another well-loved tradition was the brainchild of Dacie Moses, a former Carleton librarian. Moses often invited students to her home for fresh-baked cookies. On her death in 1981, Moses willed her house to the college, with the proviso that the ingredients for baking cookies always be kept on hand. Nowadays, any student who gets the urge for a fresh treat can go to the Dacie Moses House and bake to his or her heart's content. Under the terms of the will, leftover cookies must be left for all to enjoy.

Anyone Seen Our Bust?

And then, there's "Schiller." This tradition began in 1957, when a student stole the bust of 18th-century German poet Friedrich Schiller from Carleton's Gould Library. The student put the bust on display in his dorm room, but another student soon stole the ill-gotten gains from him.

This started a tradition of serial misappropriation of the statue. As the thievery continued, rules evolved. For example, the statue's possessor must display it publicly at least once a year and must accompany the display by the triumphant shout, "Schiller!" Also, anyone who takes possession of the statue has to sign it. In 2000, the students gave President Bill Clinton the bust when he spoke at their graduation. Clinton took the statue to Washington, signed it, and returned it. Soon after, Schiller went missing yet again.

Saint Olaf College: Early Morning Softball

Saint Olaf College is known for its music program. The school's choir is considered one of the best in the country, and in 1906, Saint Olaf's was the first American collegiate musical ensemble to perform in another country. But Olafians aren't all work and no play. In fact, in the spring, the school has a unique tradition that combines two favorite pursuits—music and sports. It's called Early Morning Softball.

They're not kidding about the "early" part. At 6:15 A.M., members of various musical organizations assemble on the football fields to compete in a softball tournament. Teams include Band, Choir, Orchestra, Norseman Band, Philharmonia, Chapel Choir, and Cantorei. Various matchups ensue, but the highlight of the tournament comes when rivals Band and Orchestra play the Broken Bat Softball Game, after which the winner takes the "broken bat" trophy for the year.

For college sports rivalries, turn to page 254.

DID YOU KNOW?

In 1921, Sister Carmela Hanggi, principal of a Catholic school in Saint Paul, founded the School Safety Patrols, a group that enlisted the aid of older students to help younger ones cross the street before and after school. A year later, the city's police chief organized patrol groups in 86 public and private schools around town. Since then, millions of elementary and middle school children have participated in the patrol program that now includes both walking and bus patrols.

The Lake Effect

Land of 10,000 Lakes? We think not! There are actually 15,291 lakes in Minnesota. How well do you know them? Take our quiz and find out.

1. What is Minnesota's deepest natural lake?
    A. Lake Saganaga
    B. Lake Vermilion
    C. Lake Minnetonka

2. Of Minnesota's 87 counties, how many have no natural lakes?
    A. Eight
    B. Four
    C. Zero

3. What is the smallest Minnesota lake?
    A. Brownie Lake
    B. Otter Tail Lake
    C. Mud Lake

4. What lake has the most shoreline?
    A. Lake Minnetonka
    B. Leech Lake
    C. Lake Vermilion

5. The largest lake is
   A. Lake Kabetogama
   B. Red Lake (Upper and Lower)
   C. Lake Winnibigoshish

6. Minnesota has how many total miles of shoreline?
   A. 90,000
   B. 110,000
   C. 75,000

7. The most common lake name in Minnesota is
   A. Goose Lake
   B. Round Lake
   C. Mud Lake

8. Lakes take up how many acres of land in Minnesota?
   A. 1,562,401
   B. 2,560,299
   C. 3,561,342

Answers on page 306.

DID YOU KNOW?

America's oldest magic store, the Eagle Magic and Joke Store, is on 4th Avenue in Minneapolis. The store has been selling magical supplies since 1900.

Odds Are It Happened in Minnesota

Lord Byron once said that truth is stranger than fiction. Here, Uncle John offers some of the strange, but true, stories to come out of Minnesota.

"Feline" Homesick

That's what Skittles the cat was in the fall of 2001. The orange-and-white cat from Kelly Lake, Minnesota, got lost on a visit to Wisconsin, where his owner and her son had been working for the summer. School was starting for Jason Sampson, and he and his mother had to return home even though Skittles had disappeared. Not to worry. Neither sleet nor mosquitoes nor the wilds of Minnesota could stay Skittles's mission: He wanted to go home. And so he did. In January 2002, 353 miles later and 140 days after going AWOL, Skittles walked up to the Sampson home in Kelly Lake, a "meow-valous" end to his long journey.

It's Beginning to Smell a Lot Like Skunkmas

The University of Minnesota in Minneapolis has a problem with Christmas tree poachers. Every year, thieves sneak onto the campus (or out of their dorm rooms) in the dead of night and cut down some of the school's pine trees. In 2002, poachers took the tops of several ancient trees, probably disfiguring the trees for life. In 2003, grounds superintendent Les Potts had had enough. He decided to have everything that might pass as a Christmas tree sprayed with a skunk scent. The "pee-ew" perfume would be dormant in the cold, but when the balsam burglars took their loot into a warm home, they'd be in for a surprise: The fragrance would be released, and it would smell like a live skunk was on the loose. Potts did admit that he worried about how the campus would smell come summertime, but drastic situations called for drastic measures. The University of Minnesota was determined to save its trees. They have had some success. Since the program was instituted, only one tree has gone missing, as compared with seven in 2002.

Sickness by Potato?

In March 2003, the FBI and postal inspectors were called to a post office near Minneapolis, where a postal employee claimed to have experienced headaches and a burning sensation after handling an envelope containing a white substance. Even the ER where the employee was taken had to be shut down during the investigation. As it turned out, the envelope, addressed to California Congressman Dana Rohrabacher, contained a slice of a rotten potato and a note telling him to "have a french fry." Assuming it was a political comment on the House of Representatives changing its cafeteria menus to list "freedom fries" instead of french fries, no charges were filed. Besides, it's not illegal to send rotten food through the mail.

The Play's the Thing

In March 2003, police officers pulled unidentified remains

from the Mississippi River near Saint Paul. The remains were those of theater director Timothy Lee, who had been missing for months. Lee's death turned out to be an accidental drowning, but in an example of life imitating art, one of the plays he had recently produced for the Outward Spiral Theatre Company was called *Unidentified Human Remains*.

Going Against the Grain

In July 2004, farmer Gene Smallidge of Cottage Grove, Minnesota, found five mysterious circles in one of his grain fields. There appeared to be no sign of human involvement. He noted that if pranksters had dragged boards to make the circles, they would have shaken some of the grain out of the heads of the stalks. Yet, though flattened, the crop remained intact. The origin of the circles is still a mystery, but many have offered theories. A research volunteer from Massachusetts theorized that plasma vortices had formed in the air and found their way to the ground. Other scientists proposed that hot gases could form swirling patterns that might bowl over the barley. And there is always the "aliens" theory. Locals, however, suspect there is a lot of hot gas to the story.

For more odd stories, turn to page 119.

To Norway and Back

Junior high school guidance counselor Robert Asp dreamed of building a replica of the Gokstad Viking long ship (found near Oslo in 1880) and sailing it to Norway, the home of his ancestors.

If You Build It

Asp began construction in 1974, and over the years many of his neighbors, also the descendants of Scandinavian settlers, offered to help. Local lumberyards donated the wood (white oak, because it was flexible and good for ship construction). Asp also rented a former potato warehouse for $10 a year and turned it into the Hawley Shipyard. Workers removed the building's first floor so that the long ship could be built on the basement floor and wouldn't breach the ceiling.

Construction went slowly. Asp worked as a guidance counselor at nearby Moorhead Junior High, so he could only devote himself to the ship part-time. Finally, in July 1980, the boat was finished. There was just one problem. The builders had no idea how to get it out of the shipyard.

At 76 feet long and 17 feet wide, the ship certainly wouldn't fit through the front door. There was only one solution: The front wall of the shipyard would have to be torn down so the boat could be pulled out. Crews shored up the three other walls, and on July 10, they razed the front wall. The ship rolled over a gravel ramp and onto the street, where a crane picked it up and secured it on the back of a truck. A christening ceremony followed; Asp's mother-in-law christened the ship the *Hjemkomst*, meaning "homecoming" in Norwegian.

The Maiden Voyage

Now the question was whether or not the ship would float. The only way to know was to try it out. So on August 9, a crane lowered the *Hjemkomst* into Duluth Harbor. She floated, and Asp took her for a spin around the harbor. It seemed that he was on his way to achieving his dream of sailing to Norway.

But Robert Asp was a sick man. He had been diagnosed with leukemia in 1974, and he died in December 1980. His last trip on the Viking ship took place in September of that year.

To Norway!

Asp's family wasn't willing to let his dream die with him. His wife and children decided to hire a crew and sail to Norway themselves.

Training took place on Lake Superior. The Asp family enlisted the help of Erik Rudstam, a well-known and skilled Norwegian sailor. Rudstam made some small improvements on the ship to make it more stable and then declared he was ready. It was finally time to leave for Oslo.

The *Hjemkomst* left Duluth in May 1982. It sailed across Lake Huron and Lake Erie, along the Erie Canal and the Hudson River. The trip wasn't always easy. The lack of wind and currents on the canal meant that the crew had to row the long ship for several miles. But on June 8, the ship arrived in

New York City, circled the Statue of Liberty, and took to the open ocean.

She's Leaking!

About 500 miles out of New York, the *Hjemkomst* hit a storm. Thirty-foot waves and strong winds tossed the ship about, and the crew struggled to keep the vessel afloat. When the storm subsided, crew members noticed a 14-foot-long crack along the port side.

This was a crossroads for Rudstam, who was acting as the ship's skipper. Should he turn back to New York or continue on to Norway? Turning back meant fighting the wind; it could take as long to return to New York as to sail on to Norway, and there was no telling whether they'd make it to either port. He decided to keep going. The crew patched the crack with burlap sacks and sailed on.

Homecoming

By comparison, the rest of the journey was uneventful. Crew members read, listened to music, and even swam with dolphins. Then on July 19, 1982, the *Hjemkomst* arrived in the port city of Bergen, Norway. The ship and its crew had traveled 6,100 miles in 72 days. They spent the next three weeks sailing around Norway and even met with the country's king. Finally, on August 9, they arrived in Oslo. Mission accomplished.

The *Hjemkomst* spent a year in storage in Norway before a merchant ship carried it back to the United States. Today, it rests in the Heritage Hjemkomst Interpretive Center in Moorhead, Minnesota.

Let's Get Down to Business

How well do you know Minnesota's state symbols?

1. Only five states have a state muffin. Which type of muffin belongs to Minnesota?
    A. Corn
    B. Blueberry
    C. Banana nut

2. The common loon became the Minnesota state bird in what year?
    A. 1925
    B. 1899
    C. 1961

3. What is Minnesota's state butterfly?
    A. The monarch
    B. The painted lady
    C. The zebra

4. The walleye is Minnesota's state fish. What is its scientific name?

    A. *Perca fluviatilis*

    B. *Cyprinus carpio*

    C. *Stizostedion vitreum*

5. In 1984, milk became Minnesota's state drink. How many pounds of milk does the state produce annually?

    A. 9.7 billion

    B. 5.4 million

    C. 365,000

6. The state flower is the showy pink and white lady's slipper. Its plant can live up to how long?

    A. 50 years

    B. 75 years

    C. 100 years

7. The morel, Minnesota's state mushroom, is what color?

    A. Black and red

    B. Tan, brown, and gray

    C. Yellow and green

8. Minnesota's state grain, wild rice, is not related to common rice.

    A. True

    B. False

9. Who owns the copyright to the state song, "Hail! Minnesota"?

    A. The state of Minnesota

    B. The University of Minnesota Alumni Association

    C. General Mills

10. The red or Norway pine, Minnesota's state tree, begins producing cones at what age?

    A. 5 to 10 years

    B. 10 to 15 years

    C. 15 to 20 years

Answers on page 307.

DID YOU KNOW?

The Twin Cities were so named in the late 1800s. A Minneapolis newspaper ran a story saying that the city should incorporate nearby Saint Paul and rename it South Minneapolis. Residents of Saint Paul, a city in its own right and one with its own personality and culture, protested and insisted that the cities stay autonomous. To make sure that everyone knew Minneapolis and Saint Paul were two distinct places, people started to call them the "Dual Cities." That moniker later evolved into the "Twin Cities."

Toys on a LARK

In this store, a big kid at heart is running the show.

Walking into the LARK toy store in Kellogg, Minnesota, is like stepping into Toyland. A playful wooden troll named Kral (LARK spelled backward) watches from the rafters. A glass display case shows off model ships and lead toy soldiers. A toy train runs on a track overhead. Rooms overflow with wooden toys, antique toys, and rare children's books.

The store's name is an acronym for Lost Arts Revival by Kreofsky, and it's the brainchild of artists Donn and Sarah Kreofsky. The two have been selling handmade and unique toys since 1983.

The Boy Who Would Be LARK

Donn Kreofsky's love of toys began in Plainview in the early 1950s when polio confined him to bed. He was quarantined to stop the spread of the disease and played alone with a collection of toy soldiers throughout his long recuperation. As he got older, he also developed his artistic side, drawing or painting while other kids at school took part in PE. In college, Kreofsky studied art at the University of Minnesota and then taught art at Winona State University and Saint Mary's College. But it wasn't until he married Sarah and they had three children that his artistic side combined with his toy-loving side; the first pieces he made for his sons were a wooden turtle, flamingo, and Noah's ark on wheels. From there, he started making toys for sale, and the rest is history.

Today, the Kreofskys' store is a multiroom affair. The 31,500-square-foot building hosts the largest specialty toy seller in North America. More than 192,000 different kinds of toys are on sale in seven themed rooms:

- Merlin's Toys, a room filled with kites, magic sets, telescopes, rock polishers, and more.
- Baby Boomer Heaven, where adults (and their kids) can find more than 500 kinds of classic toys, including lead soldiers, windup toys, and die-cast cars.
- End of the Tale Books, a room filled with new and classic children's books like *The Boxcar Children* and *Snip, Snap, Snurr.*
- Geppetto's Toys, where you'll find Donn's LARK-designed wooden toys.
- Chagall's Studio, a place to find art and craft supplies and projects.
- Magic Troll Toys, if you're looking for hand puppets, dolls, and stuffed animals.
- Potter's Toys, where you'll find card games, board games, and puzzles.

Spin Me Right Round

By far, though, LARK's biggest draw is a handcrafted carousel that took Donn and his creative team nine years to create. The carousel has made LARK a must-see stop for visitors through-out the Midwest.

The carousel opened in 1998, and during its first weekend, 8,500 people came by. It's 30 feet across, weighs 23,500 pounds, and costs $1 to ride. The carousel sports 19 animals and a wheelchair chariot all made from kiln-dried basswood, chiseled, sanded, painted, and brushed with a polyurethane finish to help withstand the wear of countless riders. Donn designed each animal himself, and many were inspired by his Minnesota surroundings: a white-tailed deer stands 43 inches tall and carries a blue jay on its back; a Minnesota river otter wears a saddle whose buttons are made from shells found on the shores of Lake Pepin; and an elegant white swan turns to check that her rider is comfortable on a lily pad saddle. The carousel's signature piece, though, is a green and orange dragon. A blue-robed wizard holding a scepter rides on the animal's back, and red flames curl from the dragon's nostrils. To make a carousel ride at LARK even more exciting, a colored fiber-optic system on the ceiling simulates the Northern Lights.

Fun Facts:

- LARK also has a toy museum inside the store. There, Donn displays the 20,000 toys he's collected over the years, including toy robots, antique cars, and old board games.
- LARK's mascot and resident pet is a potbellied pig named Gip ("pig" spelled backward).

Home on the Range

Minnesota's mines traveled a rocky road to success.

At the end of the Civil War, northeastern Minnesota was a vast wilderness. By 1900, though, the area had been transformed and had become one of the most valuable mining regions in the United States.

Men of Iron

Change arrived in northeastern Minnesota in 1865 in the form of George Stuntz, a prospector and government surveyor. Stuntz came to Lake Vermilion (near what is now the town of Tower) in search of gold. Instead, he found a rich deposit of iron ore in the Vermilion Iron Range.

Five percent of the earth's crust contains iron, but finding rocks made up of more than 50 percent iron (called hematite) that are also large enough to mine economically is rare. The beds of hematite Stuntz found near Lake Vermilion were hundreds of feet high and over the next 80 years yielded more than 15 million tons of ore.

In 1890, another prospector, Leonidas Merritt, found an iron range that overshadowed the Vermilion. Merritt and his brothers were prospecting on the west end of the Mesabi hills that stretch from Grand Rapids to Babbitt, Minnesota. There, they found the Mesabi's first beds of marketable iron ore: 110

miles long, one to three miles wide, and 500 feet thick.

Then, in 1903, prospector Cuyler Adams, accompanied by his dog Una, was surveying land southwest of the Mesabi when he discovered yet another iron range near Deerwood, Minnesota. Named for Cuyler and Una, the Cuyuna Range was exporting iron by 1911.

Together, the Vermilion, Mesabi, and Cuyuna, all located in northeastern Minnesota, took on the nickname "the range."

Making Change

Methods for extracting iron from the range varied. When the ore was buried deep below the surface, as was the case in the Vermilion, miners dug shafts and horizontal subterranean tunnels called "drifts" to reach it. Shafts sometimes dropped half a mile through solid rock down to drifts that ran a mile long. In the Mesabi and parts of the Cuyuna, the ore was closer to the earth's surface, and miners used steam shovels to extract it. At the Hall Rust Mine, an open-pit mine outside of Hibbing, miners created a three-mile-long, two-mile-wide, 60-foot-deep canyon from which to remove ore.

As the mines got going, workers poured into the area. The majority were immigrants from Europe. They settled near the mines, forming communities that began as rows of tar-paper shacks but eventually grew into towns like Eveleth, Chisholm, Virginia, and Hibbing.

New transportation lines followed. Roads, railroads, and port terminals were built to connect the range with distant steel mills in Ohio and Pennsylvania. Suddenly, northeastern Minnesota was booming.

Mining Ain't for Sissies

Mining was hard work. Workers used pickaxes and dynamite to remove the ore from rocks. Then they shoveled the ore into carts pulled by horses and mules or railroad cars that they pushed themselves.

Underground, the miners worked in damp, dark conditions. Only the flickering candles on their helmets lit their way, and often the drifts were too cramped for them to stand up straight. Workdays were long; in the early 1900s, miners worked 10-hour shifts, six days a week. In 1900, the average pay in the Vermilion was about $2 a day, a good wage for its time. But after paying the mining company for the equipment they used—everything from candles to blasting supplies—miners sometimes ended up owing the company money at the end of the month.

The work was also dangerous. Floods, cave-ins, and falling rocks were risks of the job. In 1924, Cuyuna's Milford Mine— where 48 miners were working 175 feet underground—flooded with water from nearby Lake Foley. All but seven of the men died in that disaster, often called Minnesota's worst mining accident.

Boom!

Despite the dangers, mining proved profitable. By the early 1930s, more than half of the world's iron ore came from Minnesota. That iron helped to produce everything from cars to skyscrapers. During World War I and World War II, steel made with Minnesota iron was used to build tanks, ships, and planes. In fact, an estimated 70 percent of the iron ore used to make World War II steel came from the Mesabi Range. And iron ore tonnage exported from Minnesota more than doubled between 1939 and 1941, from 18 million to 37 million tons.

A Crushing Victory

After World War II, Minnesota mines continued to prosper, but in 1951, many miners suddenly found themselves without jobs as mines started closing. Fifty years of mining had depleted much of the Vermilion's and Cuyuna's ore. The Mesabi still held a lot of iron, but it was deposited in low-grade rock called taconite. High-grade ore was more than 60 percent pure iron, whereas taconite was only about 30 percent pure. Worse, the taconite was scattered in small amounts throughout the rock, making it difficult and expensive to extract the iron.

Some people had seen this problem coming. In the 1940s, Dr. E. W. Davis, a University of Minnesota professor, started experimenting with extracting iron from taconite. By the early 1950s, his team had developed an economical way to do it. Machines crushed the taconite, removed iron ore magnetically, and then formed the ore into pellets. The remaining "impure" rock, a powder called "tailing," was discarded. In 1956, the Reserve Mining Company built the first successful taconite processing plant at Silver Bay, Minnesota. By the late 1950s, iron mines along the range were shipping taconite to the processing plant and producing 6 million to 10 million tons of iron pellets a year.

Back to Basics

Today, the Mesabi produces about 75 percent of all domestic iron ore, but over the last 50 years, Minnesota's mining industry has continued to see cycles of boom and bust. For instance, competition from international mines lowered demand for Minnesota ore in the late 1990s, but by 2004, Minnesota mining rebounded as China and other Asian countries began buying more and more iron pellets to fuel their growing industries. Still, folks on the range started looking for new ways to stay employed.

One way was to capitalize on the area's wilderness. Pristine lakes, deep woods, and even the long snowy winters have fueled a growing tourist industry. Visitors now come to the range to see wildlife, play golf, hike, bike, snowboard, and ski.

Even the mines themselves have become tourist attractions. Many former pit mines are now clear lakes filled with trout, bass, and walleye. And some underground mines, like the Soudan Mine near Lake Vermilion, offer tours so that Minnesotans and visitors can learn about the state's mining history.

To read about the haunted Milford mine, turn to page 210.

DID YOU KNOW?

The word *mesabi*, for which the Mesabi Range is named, is an Ojibwa term that means "sleeping giant."

Teensy Tenney

Now that's one small town!

Town: Tenney
Location: Wilkin County
Current population: 6
Size: 10.41 acres
Median age: 61 years

Claims to Fame:
- Tenney calls itself the smallest town in the United States.
- Between 1990 and 2000, Tenney's population increased by 50 percent (from four to six people).
- The town's official bird is the great horned owl.
- Tenney's mayor makes $96 per year and is responsible for lawn care and snow removal on public and private properties.

Meet Eugenie Anderson

One of Minnesota's most accomplished daughters is also one of America's least-discussed politicians. Biographies of Eugenie Moore Anderson rarely appear in history books, but Uncle John has compiled this list of facts to highlight her extraordinary life and career.

Starting Out

- Helen Eugenie Moore was born in Iowa on May 26, 1909. She became a full-fledged Minnesotan in 1930, when she married Red Wing resident John Pierce Anderson, son of Alexander Anderson (who invented puffed rice cereal in 1901).

- Eugenie Anderson's interest in politics began in 1937, with a visit to pre–World War II Europe. She wanted to see what was brewing on the continent and was shocked by what she discovered. In particular, she was horrified by a parade of uniformed five-year-old German boys marching in time. The trip spurred her to action; when she arrived home, she joined the League of Women Voters, the first political group to which she belonged.

Becoming a Political Powerhouse

- Anderson's parents were Republicans, but as an adult, she became a New Deal Democrat. She disdained isolationism and thought America's returning to that stance after World

War II would be disastrous. As a result, she got involved with the newly formed Democratic-Farmer-Labor Party and, in 1944, served as campaign manager for the candidate trying to unseat a local Republican isolationist congressman. While planning the campaign, Anderson consulted Minnesota Democrat Hubert Humphrey, whom she'd heard speak on the radio. Anderson's candidate ultimately lost the political race, but she formed a friendship with Humphrey that lasted for decades.

- Anderson helped Humphrey with his speech at the 1948 Democratic Convention. She suggested rewording the speech so Humphrey could advocate civil rights without seeming to oppose President Harry Truman, who didn't want to make civil rights an issue. Anderson's advice led to Humphrey making one of the most famous statements of his career, saying the Democrats should "get out of the shadow of states' rights and walk forthrightly into the sunshine of human rights."

Diplomacy Is the Spice of Life

- In October 1949, President Truman named Eugenie Anderson ambassador to Denmark, making her the United States' first female ambassador.
- Anderson was a hit with the Danes. She enrolled her children in Danish-speaking schools and learned the language herself, something ambassadors of the time rarely did. She also advanced American interests. She pushed the Danish government to take an active role in NATO and, in 1951, helped negotiate the Greenland Agreement, which allowed the

United States to use Danish air bases on the island. She worked to create a friendship treaty between the Danes and the Americans and then became the first American woman to sign a treaty when it was authorized. She served as ambassador until 1953, when Republican Dwight Eisenhower took over as president.

- When Democrat John F. Kennedy became president in 1961, Anderson once again entered politics as a diplomat. From 1962 to 1964, she served as U.S. envoy (a position similar to ambassador) to Bulgaria, and was the first American female politician to go behind the iron curtain.

Later Years

- Anderson filled the last three decades of her life with more political work. She helped Hubert Humphrey with his 1968, 1970, and 1972 presidential and senatorial campaigns. She represented the United States in the United Nations and was the first woman to sit on the Security Council. Eugenie Moore Anderson died on March 31, 1997.

DID YOU KNOW?

Hubert Humphrey was dedicated to the cause of civil rights. During his years as mayor of Minneapolis, he frequently dined with African American guests at local restaurants and ended segregation at bowling alleys in Minneapolis and Saint Paul.

Haunted Happenings: The Griggs Mansion

When it comes to Minnesota's haunted places, the Griggs mansion tops the rest. It's home to dozens of spooky characters and is often called the most haunted house in Saint Paul.

The Spook:

There are actually several spirits who haunt this house, including an older man, a Civil War soldier, and a young maid.

What Happened?

Built in 1883 by grocery baron Chauncey Griggs, the mansion is large; it has four floors and 24 rooms. High ceilings inside give it a cavernous feel, and tall trees and a sandstone wall surrounding the property make the home seem secluded even in the city.

Griggs lived in the house for only four years before he moved on. Since he left, it has served as a private residence, an art school, and even an apartment complex. And as the different residents have come and gone, they've all reported seeing strange sights, hearing weird noises, and having run-ins with a variety of spectral spooks.

The Maid

One of the ghosts most often reported at the Griggs mansion is that of an unnamed maid who, after breaking up with her boyfriend in 1915, hanged herself on the fourth floor landing. Since then, numerous people have seen her or felt her presence. One man said he saw her climbing the stairs to the fourth floor, headed for the rope she'd hung there. Others mention feeling an overwhelming sense of fear when they enter the fourth floor. And a reporter from the *Saint Paul Pioneer Press* who was visiting the mansion in search of paranormal activity said he heard footsteps on the stairs.

The Civil War Soldier

Chauncey Griggs, the mansion's original owner, served in the Civil War. So when Roma Harris, a spiritualist in Saint Paul, saw a shadowy male figure dressed in a blue Civil War soldier's uniform standing in the mansion's hall, she theorized that it was Griggs, returning to keep an eye on the home he'd built.

The Thin Man

No one knows who he is or how he's connected to the house, but at least two people have reported seeing a thin older man in a black suit and top hat. The first sighting took place in the 1950s, when an art teacher named Delmar Kolb moved into the mansion's front apartment. One night, Kolb woke up because he felt two cold fingers pressing on his forehead. Two nights later, he awoke to see the Thin Man standing near his bedroom wall. At first, Kolb was afraid a burglar had gotten inside, but when the Thin Man disappeared into the wall, Kolb decided it was a ghost.

The second sighting took place in 1964, after Carl L. Weschke bought the mansion. One night while he was working in the library, Weschke saw the Thin Man standing in the doorway. He tried to focus on the ghost, but after about 30 seconds, it vanished.

The Rest

Apparitions aren't the only spooky things people have encountered at the Griggs mansion. Visitors have reported hearing strange noises, including coughs and footsteps coming from empty rooms. Several residents spoke of doors opening and closing by themselves, windows that were nailed shut opening on their own, and paper bags jumping off of shelves. And one art student talked about feeling like someone was looking over her shoulder as she painted, but when she turned around to look, no one was there.

With all this activity, it's no wonder that the Griggs mansion is listed in the *National Directory of Haunted Places*. If you want to go for a visit, however, you won't be welcome. It's not only the spirits who disdain guests; the mansion remains a private residence whose current owners have no comment about all these haunted happenings and no interest in meeting up with ghost hunters.

For more haunted happenings, turn to page 210.

"Trivial" Minnesota

Minnesota, trivial? Hardly! But 17-, 35-, and 55-Across will test your knowledge of three of the state's most interesting facts. Good luck!

ACROSS

1	Shake ingredient
5	One with wanderlust
10	Some vows
14	By and by
15	Come to light
16	Singer's syllables
17	Mars candy introduced in 1937 for five cents
20	Sobieski of *Joan of Arc*
21	Trillion prefix
22	Balky beast
23	Way to storm off
25	Sees the light
27	"___ Blu Dipinto . . . "
28	Near-eternity
30	Takes wing
31	Member of the largest Roman Catholic order
34	Utopias
35	Brand name of a stereotypical wedding gift first marketed in Minnesota
37	Slender nails
39	Chop shop prop
40	Like a moonlit graveyard
41	*Fargo* word

42	Smiley title
45	Defeat by a small margin
48	Last name for Tony and Carmela
51	Low digit?
52	Easy companion
54	Gave for a time
55	Epithet for Madison, Minnesota
58	Czech composer Petr
59	Take home
60	Vegas pair
61	Criteria: Abbr.
62	Padlock parts
63	Jets decommissioned in 2003

DOWN

1	Actress Marlee
2	Answer to "Where are you?"
3	Preference maker
4	Prepared to propose
5	Like the Unknown Soldier
6	Sch. named for a televangelist
7	Ocean spray

For answers, turn to page 308.

8	*Jeopardy!* contestant
9	Noted plowman
10	Suffix with urban
11	More gloomy
12	Rowers
13	Snaky 1973 horror film
18	Wide shoe size
19	Crisp dress fabric
24	Stripling
26	Up in years
29	He was Mr. Spock
31	She played Clarice
32	Let up
33	Chelsea cheerios
35	Aimed at
36	Learned ones
37	Ladybugs and whirligigs
38	Stronghold
42	"Praying" insect
43	Short play
44	Scads
46	Robert of *Vega$*
47	Physicist Nikola
49	Play with bubble wrap
50	Attacks suddenly
53	Squeezes (out)
56	Naval academy grad.
57	Mushroom morsel

Minnesota Workers, Unite!

*In 1934, Minneapolis truck drivers confronted their employers
in an effort to win better salaries and the right to unionize.*

Go, Team, Go!

Until the mid-1930s, Minneapolis was a nonunion town.
Workers in a variety of industries had been trying to unionize
there since the late 1800s, and a few small unions did exist.
But a local organization called the Minneapolis Citizens
Alliance managed to keep them from affecting any change in
the city. Founded in 1903, the Citizens Alliance was comprised
of hundreds of employers in all types of industries. Their goal
was to keep unions out of local business and to retain the right
of companies to fire at will anyone with union ties. The city's
police, media, and politicians all supported the Citizens
Alliance, and the organization had been successful. Employers
in Minneapolis refused to recognize unions, did not allow
union leaders to speak on behalf of members, and fired workers who organized or joined unions.

Many Minneapolis workers thought that unfair, but the
city's truckers figured out a way to do something about it. In
February 1934, a group of coal drivers organized into the Local
574, a branch of the national, but loosely organized, Teamsters

Union. They decided to test the Citizens Alliance: the drivers shut down coal deliveries in an effort to win better wages. The Local 574 had only 75 members, but it was winter in Minnesota and coal heated houses. The men thought the Citizens Alliance had more to lose by fighting their strike than by giving them what they wanted. They were right. The strike lasted only two days, and the drivers got a raise.

Who's Running This Show?

The men in charge of the Local 574 (people like Carl Skoglund, Farrell Dobbs, and Grant Dunne) were militants. They ignored local rules and regulations in favor of dramatic strikes that railroaded employers into acquiescing. Their success with the coal drivers inspired many Minneapolis truckers in other industries to join them.

Strike!

In 1934, Minneapolis truckers made only about 20 cents an hour, and the Local 574 wanted to change that. They also wanted to break the Citizens Alliance's stranglehold on the city. So between February and May 1934, Skoglund, Dobbs, and other leaders of the Local 574 started planning for a strike of the city's truck drivers. They rented a hall to serve as headquarters for the upcoming strike. They hired people to staff the hall. And they enlisted the support of local farmers and unemployed city residents. It was the height of the Great Depression, after all; people throughout the United States were unemployed, struggling, and willing to align themselves with groups trying to improve workers' salaries. Minneapolis was no different.

On May 16, members of the Local 574 threatened to strike unless employers recognized their union, allowed union officials to represent them, and gave them a raise. The trucking companies refused, and the strike began.

Things Get Ugly

The effort immediately shut down commercial trucking all over the city. Strikers closed the downtown Central Market, where most goods going into Minneapolis were unloaded. By shutting down the Central Market, the union crippled food distribution throughout Minneapolis.

Five days into the strike, things turned violent. Armed police officers clashed with club-wielding strikers trying to stop trucks from getting to the Central Market. Thirty police officers and dozens of strikers were injured. The next day, 20,000 strikers descended on downtown Minneapolis, and the fighting continued. By day's end, three people had been killed.

You Can't Handle the Truce!

The violence led union leaders and employer representatives to begin mediation. On May 25, they signed a truce agreement that said the truckers would go back to their jobs if employers reinstated the striking workers, recognized the union, and agreed not to discriminate against workers who joined unions. Wage increases remained an issue, but the two sides decided to continue negotiating. Members of the Local 574 went back to their jobs.

The truce held for a time, but it soon appeared to the workers that employers were reneging on the deal. Union leaders and members had understood that all striking workers would be reinstated; this included the truckers, the loaders, and the "inside workers," people who staffed the warehouses. The trucking companies, however, refused to recognize inside workers as part of the agreement, a fact that so infuriated union members, they resumed the strike on July 17.

The Shot Heard 'Round the Union

Union leaders wanted a more peaceful strike this time and told picketers to leave their weapons at home. The police weren't under the same restriction. On July 20, armed with shotguns and riot gear, police officers opened fire on unarmed strikers picketing at the Central Market. Two people were killed and 50 were wounded.

In response, Minnesota's governor declared martial law and sent in the National Guard. He outlawed picketing in Minneapolis and said that trucks could move in and out of the city only if they had a military permit and escort. Guardsmen also raided the union's headquarters and arrested several leaders, imprisoning them in a stockade at the Minnesota fairgrounds. Farrell Dobbs and Grant Dunne escaped the raid and vowed to continue the strike.

It was a powerful stand, but both sides were exhausted. Dobbs and Dunne did keep the strike going for three more weeks, but everyone wanted resolution. That finally came with another mediation agreement in August 1934. The truckers would go back to work if the trucking companies recognized the union, allowed union representatives inside the company, included inside workers, and increased the workers' wages to

52 cents per hour. It was exactly what the truckers had wanted all along.

Striking Gold

The hard-fought battle of the Local 574 had a tremendous impact on labor rights and politics in Minnesota and nationwide. For its part, the Teamsters Union gained national credibility and went from a small, loosely organized group to one of the most powerful unions in the country. The Citizens Alliance was no more, and workers in all areas of industry started to unionize in Minneapolis.

On a national scale, the 1934 strike—along with similar violent confrontations in San Francisco, California, and Toledo, Ohio—inspired President Franklin D. Roosevelt to push for passage of the National Labor Relations Act in 1935. The law continues to protect the right of American laborers to form unions (except in the case of employees who work in government or the airline, railroad, and agriculture industries) and ensures that employers cannot fire workers who choose union membership.

DID YOU KNOW?

The Teamsters' name reflects its early years as a union that represented delivery drivers who commanded teams of oxen or mules. Over the last century, the group expanded to include truck drivers, chauffeurs, warehouse workers, and others. Today, the Teamsters (officially called the International Brotherhood of Teamsters) is one of the largest unions in the United States and represents more than 1 million workers nationwide.

Minnesota Curio, Part I

Minnesota boasts some of America's most interesting attractions. Uncle John has combed the countryside and compiled this list of favorites.

World's Largest Ear of Corn, Rochester

Ah, corn. That Midwest staple. Rochester's giant monument to maize, the half-husked corn tower, was built in 1932 and holds 50,000 gallons of water. From the bottom of the tower to the light atop the ear of corn, it stands 151 feet high. The ear of corn itself is 60 feet tall, making it even larger than its rival, a corn-on-the-cob gazebo in Olivia that stands about 25 feet tall.

Step Inside a Muskie, Bena

Have you ever wondered what it would be like to stand inside the mouth of a muskie? In Bena, Minnesota, you can climb inside and even have your picture taken. This muskie is a 15-foot wide, 65-foot long building that was once a hamburger stand. It's now a roadside attraction and storage unit for the gas station next door.

Bena's muskie isn't the only giant fish in Minnesota. Garrison's 15-foot walleye, Erskine's 20-foot concrete northern pike, Madison's 25-foot cod (named Lou T. Fisk, but pre-lye), and Nevis's world's largest tiger muskie are hard to ignore.

Willie the Worm Man, Pelland Junction

Six feet tall and already dangling from a hook, Willie the Worm Man might be the perfect bait for one of those monstrous fish above. If you go looking near the "Y" Bar in Pelland Junction, you'll find Willie, a chainsaw sculpture carved out of wood. He's yellow and brown, a bit cross-eyed, and has a human look to his face . . . in an oddly misshapen sort of way. He's also only a few miles from the Canadian border, so if you drop in during the winter, bundle up. Nearby International Falls calls itself one of the coldest spots in the mainland United States and has an average annual temperature of only 37.5 degrees. Brrrr . . . hanging with this Willie can get really chilly!

The Big Ball of Twine, Darwin

No longer technically "the world's largest," but it's still pretty darn impressive. Darwin native Francis Johnson started winding twine in 1950, when he twisted the first bits around two fingers. The winding continued for the next 39 years but was no easy task. As the ball grew, Frank had to come up with ways to maneuver it. At one point, he used railroad jacks to move it, and eventually, he used a crane to suspend it from the ground so that he could keep the ball round. When it got too big for the house, Frank moved the ball to his front yard where it sat until his death in 1989. Frank left his twine ball to the city of Darwin, and today, it's on display in a gazebo in the town park. Frank's ball of twine weighs 17,400 pounds; it measures 12 feet in diameter and 40 feet around. In 1991, the *Guinness Book of World Records* named the ball the largest in the world. In the years since, a ball in Kansas has overtaken the title. However, there are rumors that the Kansas ball isn't nearly as heavy or densely packed and that it contains plastic. So purists (OK, Minnesotans) maintain that the ball of twine in Darwin is still the world's largest. Since 1990, Darwin residents have celebrated Johnson's twine with the Twine Ball Days festival, held every second Saturday in August.

World's Largest Prairie Chicken, Rothsay

Once home to the state's largest population of prairie chickens, Rothsay is now home to the state's largest prairie chicken, a cement-and-steel bird built by a onetime trucker named Art Fosse. Though his name implies otherwise, Fosse never considered himself a true artist, just a guy who's good with a blowtorch. The bird he built back in the 1970s stands 13 feet tall and weighs 9,000 pounds. In case you're counting, that's about 8,998 pounds more than a real prairie chicken.

World's Largest Snowman, North Saint Paul

It's actually a stuccoman, but who's going to tell? This three-balled frigid fellow is the proud symbol of the city of North Saint Paul. A local businessman designed the more than 40-foot-tall, 2-ton, stucco-over-steel snowman, and local businesspeople coughed up the money to pay for him. Except for his height and his weight and the fact that he's not actually made of snow, the North Saint Paul snowman follows your basic design: two larger balls serve as his body, and the smallest one becomes his head, complete with a black top hat.

For more attractions, turn to page 232.

The Miracle on Ice

In 1980, with the cold war still raging, a team of young American hockey players led by a brash Minnesotan traveled to the Olympics and made history by beating an unbeatable Soviet team.

In 1999, *Sports Illustrated* magazine called the 1980 U.S. Olympic hockey team's triumph over the Soviets America's greatest sports achievement of the 20th century. The Soviets had dominated the sport internationally for two decades. Defeating them, not to mention winning the gold medal, seemed an improbable undertaking. But in the late 1970s, a college coach from the University of Minnesota decided he was going to do just that.

Assembling the Winning Team

Herb Brooks was born in Saint Paul in 1937. He fell in love with hockey at a young age, played throughout his time at Johnson High School, and then went on to play for the University of Minnesota. He also dreamed of the Olympics, and in 1960, Brooks was the last player cut from a team that went on to win a gold medal. He made the 1964 and 1968 Olympic teams, but gold medals eluded him both years. During the 1970s, Brooks coached at the University of Minnesota, where his team won three NCAA titles.

In 1979, Herb Brooks took a job as coach of the U.S. Olympic hockey team. He had a reputation for being confrontational, for pushing his players hard, and for assembling winning teams—just what the Americans needed. In the past, the Americans' way of putting together an Olympic hockey team was to pick a group of players quickly and send them off to games where they faced European and Soviet teams that had been playing together for months. It was no wonder the Americans couldn't win, and even though expectations among the Olympic committee members were low, they hoped Herb Brooks could change that.

During the spring and summer, Brooks assembled a team of 20 unknown players, nine of whom were from the University of Minnesota (another three were from the state). The others came from schools in Massachusetts, Wisconsin, North Dakota, and Ohio. Many of the players weren't the fastest or even the most skilled, but they were, Brooks contended, the "right" ones. The roster included names like Ken Morrow, Mark Johnson, Neal Broten, Mike Ramsey, and Jim Craig. Few people had heard of any of them.

In putting together his young team, Brooks was taking a chance, but he was also playing by the rules. In the 1980s, Olympic teams were supposed to be made up only of amateurs. The Soviets, however, had long been criticized for using professional players. In 1972, Canada even boycotted the hockey event at the Winter Olympics, citing that very violation. The Soviet machine simply barreled ahead, uninterested in Western opinion, an attitude that made for both a winning Olympic team and a sports rivalry between the superpowers.

Training for the Olympics

With his team assembled, Brooks began training sessions in Minnesota and set up a grueling exhibition schedule. He ran his players hard, both physically and emotionally. He made players participate in exhausting drills, changed their positions, and baited them with comments like "You don't have enough talent to win on talent alone" and "You can't be common because the common man goes nowhere. You have to be uncommon." His tactics were harsh, but players on the 1980 team still credit his aggressive style and seemingly impossible demands for their Olympic win.

As the team prepared for its Olympic run, politics over-shadowed sport, and the United States found itself in the midst of several crises. Inflation and high interest rates were choking American consumers. In November 1979, Islamic terrorists stormed the U.S. embassy in Iran and took 66 people hostage. And in December, the Soviet Union invaded Afghanistan, prompting President Jimmy Carter to announce that the United States would boycott the 1980 Summer Olympics in Moscow. This worried Brooks and his team, who were looking forward to a matchup with their famed rivals. Would the Soviets pull out of the winter games in protest?

Of course not. They had a hockey gold medal to win.

"It's Our Time"

The 1980 Winter Olympics took place in Lake Placid, New York. Despite months of training and big talk, no one on the team, including Herb Brooks, actually expected to win a gold medal. After a sound defeat (10–3 in favor of the USSR) at an exhibition game in New York City only days before the Olympics began, the American players didn't have high hopes for beating the Soviets. Brooks told his team the bronze medal was within their reach, and goalie Jim Craig commented before the first game that "the biggest game of the tournament is us against Sweden." As the Olympics got under way, though, and the Americans tied or defeated opponent after opponent, it soon became clear that they were going to play the Soviets— and that they had a real shot at the gold medal.

After a week of play, four hockey teams qualified for the semifinal medal round: the Soviet Union, Canada, Finland, and the United States. In the first game, to determine who would play for the gold, the Americans had to face the Soviets. Before the game, Brooks talked to his team. Instead of baiting them, he encouraged them. He said, "You were meant to be here . . . The moment is yours . . . It's our time." His amateur players were about to meet the professional Soviets in the most important hockey game of their lives.

USA vs. USSR

The game took place on February 22, 1980, and the Americans showed promise from the start. The Soviets scored the first goal, but as the first period wound down, the U.S. team was behind only 2–1. Even so, the Americans didn't want to end the period down a point. At the buzzer, center Mark Johnson found his mark and tied the game.

At the start of the second period, the Soviet coach made a decision that puzzled everyone. He pulled his star goaltender, Vladislov Tretiak, and replaced him with backup goalie

Vladimir Myshkin. Years later, the Soviet coach suggested that the move was a result of pressure from Soviet officials watching the game. But at the time, Brooks, his players, and even the Soviet team were confused by the decision. Regardless, it seemed to spur the Soviets to play harder. They scored again and finished the second period ahead, 3–2.

The final period began with the Americans still in the game but having been outshot 30–10. Although the entire U.S. team was playing hard, goaltender Jim Craig kept them all alive. He got some help when a power play allowed the Americans to tie the game. And then, with a 25-foot wrist shot from left wing Mike Eruzione, the Americans were up 4–3.

But there were still 10 minutes left. The Soviets had plenty of time to tie the game or even to win. Eruzione said later, "It was the longest 10 minutes of my life." Brooks's team played smart hockey, however, and the minutes counted down to seconds until sportscaster Al Michaels delivered his historic announcement: "Do you believe in miracles? Yes!"

A Gilded Ending

The United States had won. The players celebrated. The Lake Placid crowd erupted into cheers and poured onto the ice. One fan draped an American flag over Jim Craig's shoulders.

But there was still one more game to play. The Americans had beaten the Soviets, but they had not yet won the gold. That came two days later when they played Finland. Brooks was less reassuring during that pre-game pep talk. He told his players, "If you lose this game, you'll take it to your . . . grave." His team did not disappoint. After a tense and well-played game, the United States came from behind in the final period to beat Finland 4–2 and win the gold medal.

Where Are They Now?

Out of the 20 players on the 1980 U.S. Olympic hockey team, only Ken Morrow won the NHL's Stanley Cup, four times with the New York Islanders. Jim Craig became a salesman, and Mike Eruzione works as an inspirational speaker. Craig Patrick went on to work for the Pittsburgh Penguins and helped create the template for a team that won back-to-back Stanley Cups in the early 1990s. Mark Johnson had a strong NHL career with the New Jersey Devils and later became an assistant coach for the University of Wisconsin women's hockey team. Mike Ramsey, Neal Broten, Mark Pavelich, Dave Christian, Jack O'Callahan, Steve Christoff, Rob McClanahan, Dave Silk, and Bill Baker also went on to play in the NHL.

After the Lake Placid games, Herb Brooks coached the New York Rangers (1981–1985), where he reached the 100-victory mark faster than any other coach in franchise history. He also coached the Minnesota North Stars (1987–1989), the New Jersey Devils (1992–1993), and the Pittsburgh Penguins (1999–2000). He headed the French Olympic team at the 1998 Nagano games and returned to lead the U.S. Olympic hockey team to a silver medal in 2002 in Salt Lake City. Brooks died in 2003 in a car accident, but the legacy of his achievement lives on in Minnesota. In 2003, his hometown of Saint Paul erected a statue in his honor outside the Rivercentre Convention Center, and in 2006, Herb Brooks was inducted into the Olympic Hall of Fame.

Sister Kenny Tackles Polio

*As parents all over the United States kept their children
home in an effort to protect them from polio, an Australian nurse
arrived in Minnesota and brought with her a seemingly
miraculous method for treating the disease.*

From 1916 to the mid-1950s, polio was the most talked-about
disease in America. Every summer, children all over the
country developed headaches, stiff necks, and fevers that often
quickly led to paralysis and death. Polio wasn't America's most
deadly plague; many more people died of influenza and pneumonia. But it was one of the most mysterious and frightening
illnesses of the 20th century.

Lockdown

Polio primarily attacked children. For many years, it was called
"infantile paralysis" because most of its victims were between the
ages of two and six. Yet no one really knew how the disease
spread. Scientists initially suspected that it was airborne. It was
true that when one child in a town showed signs of polio, others
also came down with symptoms. So when a polio epidemic
began, everything shut down. Pools closed. Sunday school
classes were canceled. Fairs were canceled. School was canceled.

But the efforts were futile. Polio wasn't actually spread
through the air, so the quarantines were useless. People

contract polio after ingesting the virus; children might get it on their hands (and then put their fingers in their mouths) while they're outside playing or when they are sharing food. And exposure occurs weeks, sometimes months, before symptoms appear. So despite the public's best efforts, polio remained a persistent threat. In 1916, 27,000 people in 26 states contracted polio. In 1952, the height of the epidemic in America, 58,000 polio cases were reported. In Minnesota, the worst epidemic occurred in 1946, when 2,000 children in Minneapolis alone were struck with polio.

Before 1940, people with polio were treated in one of two ways. Patients who had bulbar polio, which affected the lungs and made it difficult for them to breathe, were encased (sometimes for life) in enormous ventilators called "iron lungs." Patients with paralytic polio, which affected the limb muscles, were restrained in body casts and metal braces to restrict movement; doctors believed that the muscle spasms associated with paralytic polio made the crippling aftereffects worse, so they restrained patients' movements in the hopes of minimizing permanent deformities. Their efforts were usually unsuccessful, and most people treated this way suffered withered limbs and painful muscle degeneration for the rest of their lives. An Australian nurse named Elizabeth Kenny had a different approach, and her methods proved much more successful.

Minnesota Welcomes Sister Kenny

Born in Australia in 1880, Sister Elizabeth Kenny (she wasn't a nun; "sister" is the title for "nurse" in Australia) became a "bush nurse." At that time, there were few doctors in rural

Australia, so bush nurses provided most of the medical treatment. Kenny delivered babies, set broken limbs, and examined sick children. During a visit to an Aboriginal village around the turn of the 20th century, Kenny observed tribal doctors treating a patient whom many people now believe suffered from polio. Instead of restraining the child's limbs, the Aborigines wrapped his legs in hot cloths.

In 1911, when Kenny came across another child with similar symptoms, she used the Aboriginal techniques and added some of her own. Kenny had long been fascinated by human anatomy, and her studies led her to believe that paralyzed or injured muscles could sometimes be retaught to work as they had before an injury if the muscles were made pliant enough (through heat and massage) and not allowed to waste away. So she used therapeutic exercise and massage to compliment the Aboriginal hot cloth treatment for her polio patient's paralyzed legs. The girl made a full recovery.

Kenny's approach was revolutionary. However, Australian doctors, like their American counterparts, believed in the restraint approach and scoffed at Kenny and her methods. For the next 20 years, she continued to treat Australian polio patients this way even though most of the country's medical community failed to support her. A few doctors did encourage her and urged her to move to the United States where the medical community was eager for new research into polio treatment and prevention.

So in 1940, Kenny traveled to America where, despite her high hopes, doctors in California and New York ignored her. Finally, she arrived in Minnesota, where doctors were interested in her methods and hoped to learn more about them. Her first stop was the Mayo Clinic in Rochester; from there, she moved to Minneapolis.

Helping Polio Patients to Walk

One of the first Minnesotans Sister Kenny treated was Henry Haverstock Jr., a Minneapolis teenager who contracted polio in 1939. Haverstock spent his days confined to bed, his legs and hips so immobilized with metal braces that he couldn't sit up. The first thing Kenny did after she examined the boy was to remove the braces. After a few weeks of treatments with hot packs, massage, and exercise, Haverstock was walking again.

Kenny's treatments worked, but in most cases, they were painful. Arvid Schwartz, a patient from Green Isle, Minnesota, remembered that the treatments "consisted basically of hot packs and then more hot packs. I dreaded them. They were hotter than hot, and before they cooled off, [someone would] come by and put on fresh ones."

The Institute

Shortly after her arrival in Minneapolis, Sister Kenny gave a lecture at the University of Minnesota, where she presented her rehabilitation techniques to doctors from all over the Midwest. They were skeptical, but they listened and began to use Kenny's methods to treat their own patients. By 1942, as word of Kenny's methods got around, the incidence of prolonged paralysis in people afflicted with polio had dropped from 85 percent to 15 percent.

On December 17, 1942, with the financial help of several

Minnesota doctors, Kenny opened the first Sister Kenny Institute in Minneapolis, where she and her staff treated patients and monitored their success. Even so, Sister Kenny and her methods were never fully accepted by America's governing medical body; the American Medical Association remained critical of her approach. No matter. By the mid-1940s, Kenny's methods were the most widely accepted treatment for polio in the United States.

Sister Kenny died in 1952, just three years before the introduction of the successful Salk polio vaccine. Today, thanks to vaccination programs, polio has been almost completely eradicated in the Western world.

Her Legacy

Sister Kenny couldn't cure polio. There still is no cure for the disease. And she couldn't do much for patients with bulbar polio, though she did condemn the immobilization involved with the use of iron lungs and suggested that patients be weaned off of ventilators or at least use them only sporadically. What she did was treat paralytic polio symptoms in a way that helped the body heal itself. Her methods laid the foundation for modern physical therapy, and today, the Sister Kenny Rehabilitation Institute uses her techniques to provide short- and long-term muscle rehabilitation treatment for patients at its five Minnesota locations.

Mall of America by the Numbers

Bloomington, Minnesota, is home to the largest indoor shopping mall in the United States. How big is it? Check out the numbers.

0

Heaters used to heat the main building. So many people visit the mall, and there's so much heat generated by the facilities and equipment, that the entire 4.2-million-square-foot building heats itself. Heaters are used only in the entranceways from the parking area.

4

Stories in the LEGO store, where visitors can walk among LEGO models that include dinosaurs, planets, and the world's largest animated and interactive LEGO clock tower

20

Minimum number of people needed to participate in a MallQuest Scavenger Hunt, whereby everyone in the group splits into teams of five to go on a mall-wide hunt for goodies

24

Public restrooms in which to read the *Uncle John's* series

30

Rides and amusements in The Park at MOA, the largest indoor family amusement park in the nation. Its wildest ride is the Timberland Twister, a roller coaster whose cars spin 360 degrees on the track as it rolls.

75¢

Cost of a small locker rental; a large locker costs $1.25.

76

Times the White House could fit inside the mall

520

Stores

750

Horsepower rating of the Mall's NASCAR Silicon Motor Speedway racing simulators. Amateurs can buckle into the cockpit of a virtual NASCAR machine that's so real there's even a "chicken switch" emergency turnoff in case you freak out.

4,000+

Couples who have married at the mall's Chapel of Love Wedding Chapel

11,000

Year-round employees (there are also 13,000 seasonal employees)

12,550

Parking spaces on site

79,200

Wads of gum removed from the mall's carpet to date

1 million

Total number of ladybugs released into the mall's indoor garden to help control pests

1.2 million

Gallons of water in the Underwater Adventures Aquarium. Besides being a source of fantastic fish sightings, the aquarium includes a glass-walled conference room that companies can rent for meetings of up to 100 people.

23 million

Pounds of french fries sold at mall restaurants

105.6 million

Rolls of toilet paper used in mall bathrooms since opening day in 1992

425 million+

Total visitors to date

$1.8 billion

Annual economic contribution to Minnesota's economy. That's more than the gross domestic product of Monaco, Greenland, or Samoa.

Surfing Minnesota

When someone says "surfing" and "North Shore," most people think "Hawaii." Not so in Minnesota.

Any serious Minnesota surfer knows that surfing the North Shore doesn't have to involve a plane ride or a crowded Banzai Pipeline. Storms make for some gnarly winter waves on Lake Superior. The surf season usually lasts from October to February, and waves can reach six feet high. So grab a board and wet suit, get stoked, and prepare to dodge the ice floes, because Uncle John has tracked down some of the best surf spots along Lake Superior's west coast.

Park Point, Duluth

A sandbar makes the surf at Park Point relatively gentle. The best place to catch waves here is off the canal wall, where wind, water, and wall combine to produce rideable sets.

Mouths of the French and Lester Rivers, about 15 miles north of Duluth

The cobbled lake bed at the mouths of both rivers makes for a fun, gentle surf break.

Stony Point, about 15 miles north of Duluth

Possibly the best spot along Superior's west coast, Stony Point gets some great waves and is the lake's most dependable surf spot. It has deep offshore water and generally doesn't freeze during the winter. But if you wipe out in shallow water, be careful. Hitting the lake bed's stones (which give the beach its name) can be painful.

Beaver Bay, Two Harbors

The surf can get rough here, and the high rocky cliffs make for dangerous conditions. But if you're an experienced surfer and know how to maneuver a treacherous wave, you might enjoy Beaver Bay.

Judge C. R. Magney State Park,
about 14 miles north of Grand Marais

The surf here is decent, but the coastline is rocky, making this one of the more dangerous spots to take to the water. If you still have some energy left after riding a Magney wave, you can also hike into the park and visit Minnesota's highest waterfall.

Superior Surfing Tips:

- Fresh water is less buoyant than saltwater, so it can be harder to stay up on a board. You'll need a thicker, longer board than you'd use in saltwater.
- Ocean surf generally reaches shore long before the actual storms that cause it, but on Lake Superior, the storms and surf go hand-in-hand, so be careful in the nasty weather.
- Superior's waves don't make for long rides; they generally last only about nine seconds.

- The surf on the lake is cold . . . like wicked cold. Water temperatures hover in the 30s during the winter. So you'll definitely need a wet suit, preferably one with a hood, gloves, and booties, and with material that is at least 4 millimeters thick.
- The waves on Lake Superior aren't as consistent as ocean surf. You may have to wait for several days before coming across a decent set.
- Never take the first wave. Those are usually smaller and not as well formed as what follows.
- Grommits beware. Wind, snow, ice, freezing water, storms, riptides, and no lifeguards make the novice surfer unsuited for surfing Lake Superior.

DID YOU KNOW?

Riding these waves isn't a new phenomenon. The brave and hardy have been surfing Lake Superior for almost 30 years. There are, however, few people who do it. Some estimates put the number of consistent Lake Superior surfers at only 20 to 30, meaning Minnesota is one of the few surf spots on earth where you can still ride a pristine, uncrowded wave.

Sara, We Hardly Knew You

A pillar of the community or an unrepentant terrorist?
Will the real Sara Jane Olson please stand up?

Locals in Saint Paul knew Sara Jane Olson as the wife of a doctor and the mother of three daughters. The family lived in the upscale neighborhood of Highland Park where the 52-year-old stay-at-home mom was well liked. She was a regular churchgoer, respected for her charitable work and her devotion to social causes.

So her friends and neighbors were shocked when on June 16, 1999, Olson was arrested and taken into federal custody. The homemaker was charged with possessing explosives and conspiring in the attempted murder of police officers.

A Blast from the Past

The police and FBI revealed that Sara Jane Olson was actually a criminal fugitive named Kathleen Ann Soliah. Soliah had been featured on TV's *America's Most Wanted,* and a tip had led to her discovery in Saint Paul after 23 years on the lam. Soliah, authorities said, was a member of the Symbionese Liberation Army (SLA), an extremist group that committed violent crimes in the early 1970s. In 1974, for example, SLA members made names for themselves when they kidnapped newspaper heiress Patty Hearst from her Berkeley, California, apartment. The SLA demanded that Patty's parents donate millions of dollars to feed the poor and needy in exchange for their daughter's safe return. The Hearsts complied, but Patty didn't come home. Instead, she appeared to join her kidnappers and participated in an armed robbery of a San Francisco bank that left two people wounded.

The SLA grabbed lots of headlines during the 1970s but had few followers. Their criminal actions—including the murder of Dr. Marcus Foster, the superintendent of Oakland's schools—turned many against them. So by 1974, the Symbionese Liberation Army had fewer than a dozen "soldiers." Most of those died in May when their hideout went up in flames during a shooting match with a Los Angeles Police Department SWAT team. Among the bodies was that of Angela Atwood, an SLA leader and a close friend of Kathleen Soliah.

With Friends Like These, Who Needs Enemies?

Atwood and Soliah met in Berkeley, California, in 1971. Soliah's first public support for the SLA came at a memorial rally after Atwood's death. At the rally, Soliah announced her solidarity with the remaining SLA members by declaring, "Keep fighting! I'm with you!"

Three surviving members of the SLA took her up on her pledge. Bill Harris, Emily Harris, and Patty Hearst were running from authorities when they asked Soliah for help and money. She provided both.

Despite having only a few remaining members, the SLA soldiered on with murder and mayhem. In April 1975, SLA members killed customer Myrna Opsahl while they were robbing a bank in Carmichael, California. And in August, the group rigged nail-filled pipe bombs to the undersides of two LAPD vehicles. The bombs never detonated.

On September 18, most of the remaining SLA members—including the Harrises and Patty Hearst—were arrested. Soliah, however, had disappeared.

The police continued to believe she had conspired with the other SLA members to plant the pipe bombs. A Los Angeles grand jury agreed and, in February 1977, handed down an indictment against her for the attempted bombing. With Soliah missing, though, there was no one to arrest.

Becoming Sara Jane

By the time of her indictment, Soliah had moved to Minneapolis and assumed a new identity. She took her first two names from the title of the Bob Dylan song "Sara Jane" and chose the surname "Olson" because it was common in Minnesota. As Sara Jane Olson, Soliah met and married medical intern Gerald "Fred" Petersen, and the couple settled in Saint Paul to raise their three daughters.

In Saint Paul, Sara Jane Olson lived an upper-middle-class lifestyle. She was a gourmet cook and an actress in local theater productions. She took her youngest daughter to soccer practice. She also helped the less fortunate. The pastor of her church said she kept busy by "feeding the hungry, helping to house the homeless, reading to the blind, helping people learn English as their second language." In all, Olson spent nearly 20 years in Saint Paul as a respected member of the community.

In 1999, though, Sara Jane Olson (she legally changed her name after her arrest) became the center of federal case number A325036. The doctor's wife faced life in prison, and Minnesotans were caught up in her controversy. Her family and local supporters, mindful of Olson's good deeds, believed in her innocence. They raised $1 million in bail, formed a committee to aid her defense, and even published a fund-raising cookbook of her favorite recipes: *Serving Time: America's Most Wanted Recipes*. At the same time, Olson's critics pointed to the victims of the SLA and argued that the kind and charitable Sara Jane Olson was just another role for murderess Kathleen Soliah.

The Trial That Never Was

The mystery of Olson's true nature only deepened as her case went forward. According to defense attorneys, Olson had befriended members of the SLA out of grief over the death of Angela Atwood but had never been an active member of the group or tried to harm anyone. Former SLA member Bill Harris backed up this story.

The prosecution's case was more complicated. Many judicial experts called the case against Olson weak and problematic because so many years had passed since the bombing and because two of the witnesses who testified before the 1977 Los Angeles grand jury had died. But prosecutors wanted to bring Olson to trial, and they still had one key witness whose story was powerful: Patty Hearst. In 1981, Hearst had published an autobiography entitled *Every Secret Thing*, in which she accused Soliah not only of being at the center of attempted bombings, but also at the Carmichael bank robbery where

Myrna Opsahl was killed. Hearst was prepared to testify to this at Olson's trial.

She never got the chance. After two years of protesting her innocence and calling herself the "victim of a witch hunt," Sara Jane Olson shocked her supporters on October 31, 2001, when she pleaded guilty to possessing explosives with the intent to murder. Outside the courtroom, though, she said she was innocent and had pleaded guilty only because her lawyers convinced her that the September 11 terror attacks would make it impossible for an accused bomber to get a fair trial. The presiding judge didn't believe her claims, and he sentenced Olson to imprisonment for 20 years to life; the sentence was eventually reduced to 13 years.

Then, in 2002, Olson was charged with first-degree murder for the death of Myrna Opsahl. She changed her mind about this one too. Initially, she pleaded innocent but, by November, accepted her part in the robbery that killed Opsahl; a judge added six years to her sentence for that crime. The fugitive Kathleen Ann Soliah was finally behind bars.

DID YOU KNOW?

Patty Hearst always argued that she joined her kidnappers out of fear, not allegiance. Even so, she went to trial, was convicted, and spent 32 months in jail for her part in the SLA's San Francisco bank robbery. In 2001, during his last hours in office, President Bill Clinton pardoned her.

Minnesota on the Tube

Minnesotans have lent their state and cultural personality to a number of popular television shows. Here are some of our favorites.

The Mary Tyler Moore Show, 1970–1977, CBS

For many Americans, Mary Tyler Moore put Minneapolis on the map. The show's premise was that after a failed engagement, perky Mary Richards moved to the "big city" to make a life for herself on her own, a shocking concept in the 1970s. The opening credits present Mary as a young woman "who can turn the world on with her smile," and in a famous sequence, she tosses her beret into the air on the corner of 7th Street and Nicollet Mall in downtown Minneapolis. Today, a statue of Mary stands at that very spot, and the rest of the footage in the lead-in was shot within a couple of blocks of that corner.

Producers chose Minneapolis as the setting for *The Mary Tyler Moore Show* because it offered the "big city with a small-town feel" they needed. The writers wanted a location that had the energy of a large city, one that afforded Mary the opportunity to meet many interesting people and be involved in varied activities. But they also needed it to be a place small and intimate enough that the newsroom could believably make do with just one writer, one anchorman, and one associate producer (as dictated by the number of characters on the show).

And the employees of the newsroom had to be down-to-earth enough to be chummy with the TV station's other personalities, including a cooking show host named Sue Ann Nivens and Chuckles the Clown. Plus, giving Mary midwestern roots offered a perfect contrast to the New York brashness of her upstairs neighbor, Rhoda Morgenstern.

Fun fact:

The house used as the exterior of Mary's apartment building is still standing at 2104 Kenwood Parkway in Minneapolis. It has been painted brown and is a private residence, but it's still recognizable as the house that held Mary's, Rhoda's, and Phyllis's apartments.

Little House on the Prairie, 1974–1984, NBC

For ten years *Little House on the Prairie* reigned as one of the best-loved programs on television. Loosely adapted from Laura Ingalls Wilder's autobiographical series of children's books, it recounted the story of a feisty young girl's hardscrabble but idyllic childhood on the Minnesota prairie. The real-life and fictional Ingalls families both settled on the banks of Plum Creek near the town of Walnut Grove, Minnesota. The real family stayed for only a couple of years, but the fictional Ingalls characters made a life there. The show told of the family's struggle to survive the harsh winters, crop failures, locust infestations, Indian attacks, and other problems that plagued Minnesota pioneers.

Fun fact:

The show was set in Minnesota but filmed at the Big Sky Ranch in Simi Valley, California (the same set used for shows like *Gunsmoke* and *The Dukes of Hazzard*). Keen Minnesotan eyes will catch the California mountains in the background; no such mountains exist in southern Minnesota.

The Golden Girls, 1985–1992, NBC

Although not set in Minnesota, *The Golden Girls* had strong Minnesota ties. This sitcom chronicled the lives and adventures of four women who shared a Florida house. One of them, Rose Nylund (played by Betty White), hailed from the rural Minnesota hamlet of Saint Olaf. Good-hearted but naïve, Rose always told long stories of the happenings in Saint Olaf and tried to apply them to current situations. Her friends poked fun at her stories, but the morals she espoused usually taught valuable lessons.

Fun facts:

- Rose's Scandinavian pedigree was impeccable. Her mother's maiden name was Gerkelnerbigenhoffstettlerfrau.
- In the pilot episode, Rose's hometown was said to be Little Falls, Minnesota. In subsequent episodes, it became Saint Olaf.

Coach, 1989–1997, ABC

In this series, Craig T. Nelson played Hayden Fox, the head coach of the Minnesota State University Screaming Eagles. Aided by two bumbling assistant coaches, he had to deal with a mediocre team and constant upheaval in his personal life. During the 1995–1996 season, Fox and the sitcom's primary characters abandoned Minnesota for Florida to coach a pro football team, the Orlando Breakers. The series was never the same after that and was canceled a year later.

Fun fact:

The football footage used on the show is film of actual University of Minnesota football games.

The Oldest Little Town in Minnesota

This Mississippi River town offers a mix of historic charm and quirky attractions.

Town: Wabasha
Location: Wabasha County
Founding: 1830
Current population: 2,599
Size: 9.3 square miles
Median age: 43.8
County seat: Yes

What's in a Name?

The town and county were named for a local Sioux leader, Chief Wa-pa-shaw III.

Claims to Fame:

- Wabasha is the oldest town in Minnesota. It was established officially in 1830 with a treaty, The Second Treaty of Prairie du Chien, and has been occupied continuously since 1826. However, it wasn't actually named "Wabasha" until 1843.
- The 22-room Anderson House, located on Main Street, opened in 1856 and is Minnesota's oldest continuously

operating hotel. Anderson House offers several unique amenities, including a hot brick for your feet on cold nights (hotel staff deliver the brick in a quilted envelope) and a complimentary shoeshine for any shoes left in the hall. Guests can also adopt one of the hotel's four cats during their stay (cat-free rooms are available).

- Every May, Wabasha residents participate in the 100-Mile Garage Sale. The sale lasts for three days, stretches along the Mississippi River from Red Wing to Winona, and includes 14 towns on both the Minnesota and Wisconsin sides of the river.

- American bald eagles thrive in Wabasha. The Mississippi River doesn't freeze over in the Wabasha channel, so the eagles can find fish to eat even in the dead of winter. From November to March, the eagles nest near town. Visitors hoping to catch a glimpse of America's official bird can check out the eagle watch deck at the end of Pembroke Avenue, and anyone wishing to learn more about the birds can visit Wabasha's National Eagle Center, an organization dedicated to educating the public about eagles.

- Wabasha is the setting of and inspiration for *Grumpy Old Men* and *Grumpier Old Men* (though townspeople want to make clear that they're anything but grumpy). Screenwriter Mark Steven Johnson loosely modeled the movies' main characters after the owners of Church Avenue's Slippery's Bar and Restaurant.

Six Things You Don't Know About Kevin McHale

*Hibbing's Kevin McHale delivered a slam
dunk for Minnesota basketball.*

For 13 seasons, McHale was part of the Boston Celtics' "Big Three," a formidable trio that included Larry Bird and Robert Parish. Together with their teammates, they guided Boston to nine Atlantic Division titles, six Eastern Conference titles, and three NBA championships. McHale's individual play was a big factor in the team's success, and the former Minnesota Gopher was rewarded for his efforts with seven All-Star team selections. He has since gone on to serve as general manager for the Minnesota Timberwolves.

1. His first sporting love was hockey.
Like many Minnesota boys, McHale dreamed of lacing up his skates for the North Stars. He might have, too, were it not for a growth spurt during high school that made basketball a better choice. Over a four-year span, the Hibbing High student morphed from a diminutive five-foot-nine freshman to a towering six-foot-eleven senior. His rapid height gain was all the more surprising because both of his parents were less than six feet tall.

2. In 1995, he was honored as the top player in University of Minnesota basketball history.

The University of Minnesota's basketball program has had plenty of high profile stars over the years, but when it came time to select the best, school officials chose Kevin McHale. During his four years with the team, McHale was twice named to the All-Big 10 team. He graduated as the school's second all-time leader in points and rebounds. He averaged 15.2 points and 8.5 rebounds per game over his four-year college career. And he led the Gophers to the NIT championship game during his 1980 senior season.

3. He was the first player to win the Sixth Man Award in consecutive seasons.

During the early part of his career, McHale was routinely the first player off the Celtics' bench, a vital role that earned him the reputation as the team's sixth man. "Making him the sixth man and selling him on it was important," said Bill Fitch, McHale's first coach in Boston. "You've got to have those bench points and have them every night. Kevin got them." As a matter of fact, McHale was so impressive in his role that he won the NBA's Sixth Man of the Year award for the 1983–1984 and 1984–1985 seasons.

4. He had great defensive skills.

Although largely known for his offensive play, McHale was also a lockdown defender who could always be counted on to hold his man in check. During the course of his career, he was named to the NBA All-Defensive first or second team on six occasions, and he routinely ranked among the league leaders in blocks per game.

5. He was the first player to shoot better than .600 from the floor and .800 from the free throw line in the same season.
McHale accomplished that remarkable feat during the 1986–1987 season by shooting .604 from the field and .836 from the line. His accuracy landed him his first (and only) spot on the prestigious All-NBA first team at the end of year. High shooting percentages were nothing new for McHale, though. His .554 career mark is the ninth best in NBA history.

6. He is one of the NBA's 50 greatest players.
Although he played in the shadow of Larry Bird and Robert Parrish, McHale was still a tremendous talent. The NBA recognized his contribution to the game on October 29, 1996, when they announced his inclusion on their list of the 50 Greatest Players in NBA History. The list, selected by a blue-ribbon panel of media, former players, and coaches, also included Michael Jordan, Wilt Chamberlain, and Kareem Abdul-Jabbar.

Highlights as the Timberwolves General Manager:
- The Timberwolves went to the playoffs for the first time in 1997.
- He drafted Wally Szczerbiak in 1999; Szczerbiak later played for the NBA All-Rookie first Team (1999–2000) and in the 2002 NBA All-Star game.
- In 2004, as the Timberwolves' record sank in the standings, McHale fired head coach Flip Saunders and decided to do the job himself. He led the team to a 19–12 record during the last half of the season and then turned the job over to Seattle's former assistant coach, Dwayne Casey.

Light My Way

Shipping accidents on Lake Superior prompted the construction of several lighthouses. These were an effort to guide ships through darkness, storms, and fog and were also a way to let captains know exactly where the shoreline was; in many spots, the lake bed runs right into the shore with no gradual warning. Here are some of the lighthouses that guided seamen along Minnesota's Lake Superior coast.

Minnesota Point Lighthouse

Location: Minnesota Point

Built: 1856–1858

For 30 years, the Point lighthouse guided ships through the dark, narrow entry into Superior Bay. Weather eventually destroyed the lighthouse, however, and it closed in 1888. Today, the remnants of the 50-foot red brick tower still stand at the site.

Grand Marais Lighthouse

Location: Grand Marais

Built: 1886 (rebuilt in 1922)

Although Congress allotted $6,000 in 1856 to build the Grand Marais Lighthouse, nothing came of it; the money was needed elsewhere, it seemed. Finally, in 1886, the town got its light, but the building was cobbled together in Duluth, disassembled, and then shipped to Grand Marais to be reconstructed and installed. There were problems from the start. The lantern didn't work well, the roof leaked, and the building couldn't withstand the lake storms. Finally, in 1922, the lighthouse was solidly rebuilt and electrified; in 1937, it was automated. Today it still shines, guiding recreational boaters into Grand Marais Harbor.

Two Harbors Lighthouse
Location: Two Harbors
Built: 1891–1892
In 1891, Thomas Feigh, who owned the land on which the Two Harbors lighthouse now stands, sold his property to the United States government for $1. A year later, the newly constructed lighthouse and keeper's quarters were ready for operation. Today, the light still shines in Two Harbors, operated by a computer in Duluth. The main lighthouse is a bed-and-breakfast; guests even participate in running the lighthouse during their stay. And the keeper's dwelling is open to the public for tours.

Duluth Harbor Lights
Location: Duluth
Built: 1874–1910
These three structures light the way into Duluth Harbor. The North Pier Light shines from the end of the north breakwater and marks one side of the canal. The South Breakwater Light illuminates the other side. And the Rear Range Light is located near the southern end of the lift bridge. The harbor here needs three lights because the shipping canal is difficult to navigate.

Only 300 feet lie between the rocky north and south piers. The thick fog that often descends on the harbor just makes things worse, and in the dark, ships could easily run aground or smash into the rocky shore. The Duluth Harbor Lights, however, made navigating the harbor less treacherous for seamen. Today, the lighthouses continue to direct ships into the harbor and, thus, are not open to the public.

Split Rock Lighthouse
Location: Two Beavers
Built: 1909–1910
Picturesque, famous (it was featured on a postage stamp in 1995), and perched on a 130-foot-high cliff at the edge of Lake Superior, the Split Rock lighthouse tower stretches another 54 feet to the sky. It is so high that captains on ships as far as 22 miles away could see the light. Modern navigational equipment made the lighthouse obsolete in 1969, and today it shines only on special occasions, including the anniversary of the 1975 *Edmund Fitzgerald* shipping disaster.

DID YOU KNOW?

Lake Vermillion has 1,200 miles of shoreline, the most of any lake contained completely in Minnesota.

Minnesota Public Radio

Peace, love, and commercial-free radio.

With 37 radio stations and 13.5 million listeners nation-wide, Minnesota Public Radio is not doing too badly for a former college radio station. In fact, MPR has racked up some pretty impressive stats:

- It produces more national programming than any other station-based public radio organization.
- It has the highest percentage of listener membership of any public radio network nationwide.
- It covers all of Minnesota and parts of Wisconsin, Michigan, Iowa, Idaho, the Dakotas, and Canada.
- It has won more than 800 journalism awards.

Make Radio, Not War

When talking about the history of Minnesota Public Radio, one name always comes to mind: Bill Kling. He headed the first MPR station, KSJR 90.1 FM in Collegeville, Minnesota, and still runs the network today.

MPR spun off of the college station at Saint John's University. The year was 1967. It was a time of revolution and free love, and yeah, the radio was already free, but why not a radio station free from commercials? Bill Kling and MPR were primed and ready to provide that. MPR was also a founding member of National Public Radio (NPR) and helped bring the nascent organization into being.

In its early years, MPR's most well known program was *A Prairie Home Companion,* which started broadcasts in 1974. The show remains the centerpiece of MPR's lineup.

Bill Kling brought *A Prairie Home Companion* to NPR for national distribution in 1980. NPR execs turned it down flat. They claimed the show was too hokey for a sophisticated national audience. Convinced they were wrong, Kling decided to distribute the show nationally himself, and it became a hit.

Bigger and Better

Over the years, MPR just kept growing. Today, it's home to *A Prairie Home Companion* along with *Marketplace, Pipedreams, Weekend America, Sound Money,* and 14 other national programs. The network also offers Classical 24, a subscription service that allows small radio stations to broadcast classical music 24 hours a day, 7 days a week.

MPR is not without critics. Some consider Bill Kling's business tactics to be too aggressive, a position that has led to their calling his collection of radio networks "the Klingon Empire." Purists also criticize MPR's classical music programming for offering only shorter works and pieces by well-known composers.

But the listening public doesn't seem to mind. More than 690,000 Minnesotans tune in to MPR programs every week, and the station boasts more than 83,000 members.

Stay Tuned

Most of Minnesota is covered by two, if not three, different MPR stations. One offers news and talk, one offers classical music, and one plays varied selections of local music. These stations cover more areas of the state than any other public radio station; 98 percent of Minnesotans can pick up an MPR station. So if you're going for a drive from Minneapolis to Duluth to Bemidji, even to North Dakota, rest assured you'll be able to make the trip without missing a minute of *All Things Considered*.

To read about Garrison Keillor and
A Prairie Home Companion, *turn to page 18.*

DID YOU KNOW?

In 1866, Minnesota had a gold rush, but it never quite panned out. A year before, the Minnesota State Legislature conducted a mineral survey of an area north of Duluth. Word got out that the prospector found gold near Lake Vermilion, and hundreds of people rushed into the area hoping to make a fortune. But by 1867, the Minnesota gold rush had gone bust.

Gold had indeed been found near Lake Vermilion, but it was trapped in hard quartz and bedrock and was nearly impossible for individuals to mine. Faced with a lack of easily mined gold and northern Minnesota's harsh winters, many prospectors abandoned their quests and left the state.

The Blizzard Is Coming

Snowstorms come up in Minnesota faster than a Norwegian can say "Uff Da!" And some storms take even the most prepared residents by surprise. Here are some of the state's whopper snowstorms.

The Schoolchildren's Blizzard, 1888

On January 12, 1888, Minnesota's pioneer children were hard at work at their studies. One-room schoolhouses dotted the prairie, and many children walked miles every day just to attend school. The day was unseasonably warm, and many students had left for school without mittens or heavy coats. Over the course of the afternoon, the temperature dropped significantly; in some places, it fell as much as 70 degrees. Outside, thermometers dipped below zero. Then came the snow and wind. Children in the western part of the state were trapped in their schoolhouses, and 109 people died. Some children, however, were led to safety. They held hands to form human chains or followed ropes that led them into warm stores and homes in their prairie towns.

The Armistice Day Storm, 1940

Any Minnesotan who is old enough to remember 1940 will remember the Armistice Day Storm. Monday, November 11, dawned a beautiful day. Temperatures were mild for November;

by midday, some thermometers reached 60 degrees. Minnesotans were out and about, enjoying the warm weather. At about three o'clock in the afternoon, though, everything changed. The sky darkened. A fierce, icy wind blew in from the west. Rain, then snow, began to fall. The temperature dropped 30 degrees, and winds lashed the Mississippi River and Lake Superior. Hunters and boaters caught unaware found themselves stranded.

The snow was blinding and thick, and it lasted for three days. In all, 16 inches fell on Minneapolis and 27 in Collegeville. Rescuers had to use long probes to locate cars buried in 20-foot drifts. Trains collided in the whiteout, and 49 people across the state died, many of them hunters trapped outside.

Minnesota's weathermen, it seems, were caught by surprise as much as the public. No one was watching the developing storm or following its progress. The main Midwestern meteorology center in Chicago wasn't even staffed overnight, and it issued only four forecasts per day for the nearby states of Minnesota, Illinois, Indiana, Iowa, Michigan, Wisconsin, and the Dakotas. As a result of the surprise storm, changes were made in the way meteorology offices in the area were run; the Chicago office began operating around the clock, and in the Twin Cities, the weather station was updated so it could make its own forecasts.

The Storm of the Century, 1975

It's called the "Storm of the Century" because for three days (January 10–12), snow, rain, sleet, and wind battered Minnesota. Temperatures dropped more than 30 degrees in a matter of hours. Roads were closed for 11 days. Winds gusted to 80 mph, and snow drifted 20 feet or more. International Falls recorded a snowfall of 23.5 inches.

The Halloween Blizzard, 1991

On October 31, 1991, children across the country were gearing up for a night of trick-or-treating. In Minnesota, the kids were lamenting the weather.

In southern Minnesota, the three-day blizzard that began on Halloween brought ice. Eleven central and southeastern counties were declared disaster areas due to the treacherous icy conditions. In the north, the storm brought snow. Before it was over, 28 inches of snow fell in Minneapolis–Saint Paul, and in Duluth, residents found themselves buried under 36.9 inches, a record single-storm snowfall for that city.

DID YOU KNOW?

Minnesota boasts many records and firsts when it comes to winter and snow.

- An Iowa newspaper first used the term "blizzard" in connection with weather to describe a March 14–16, 1870, Minnesota storm.
- The least snowy winter in the Twin Cities was 1930–1931, when only 14.2 total inches of snow fell.
- The snowiest winter on record for the Twin Cities is the 1983–1984, winter when a total of 98.6 inches of snow fell in Minneapolis and Saint Paul.
- In February 1996, the northeastern town of Tower boasted the coldest Minnesota temperature on record: -60 degrees.

One Heck of a Slapshot

When it comes to hockey, Eveleth scores big.

Town: Eveleth
Location: Saint Louis County
Founding: It depends on whom you ask. Many will say 1892, the year the town's plat was drawn up. But others claim the official founding was actually the next year, because no one could get to the county offices to file the plat before the spring thaw.
Current population: 3,865
Size: 6.5 square miles
Median age: 40.9 years

What's in a Name?

The town is named for Erwin Eveleth, an employee for the Robinson & Flinn timber company, which owned the land that became the town of Eveleth. Residents initially wanted to name their hamlet after Mr. Robinson, owner of the timber company, but they changed their minds because "Robinson" seemed too difficult for Scandinavian immigrants to pronounce. "Eveleth," apparently, was easier.

Claims to Fame:

- Eveleth sits in the Mesabi Range, one of the world's largest iron mining regions.

- Most visitors come to Eveleth because the town is home to the United States Hockey Hall of Fame. Established in 1983, this shrine to pucks and sticks and the folks who wield them has exhibits on everything from the early history of the game to women's hockey. And if you happened to miss the 1980 U.S. Olympic team's win over the Soviet Union or you just want to relive it, have no fear. The footage plays nonstop throughout the hall.

- The thrill of a good roadside attraction isn't lost on the people of Eveleth. They've erected a 107-foot, 7,000-pound hockey stick and 700-pound puck downtown.

- Six members of U.S. Olympic hockey teams were born and grew up in Eveleth: Andre Gambucci (1952 Olympics), Willard Ikola (1956), John Matchefts (1956), John Mayasich (1956 and 1960), Tom Yurkovich (1964), and Mark Pavelich (1980).

- Eveleth was a filming location for the 2005 movie *North Country*. The film was a fictionalized account of the first-ever class action sexual harassment lawsuit, *Jenson v. Eveleth Taconite Co.* The 1993 ruling made employers liable for the actions of their employees at work and required companies to educate workers about sexual harassment.

Odds Are, Part II

Uncle John continues its look at some of the strangest stories
to come out of Minnesota. (Part I begins on page 44.)

Ask and Ye Shall Receive

After an August 2004 sermon on stealing, Saint Paul pastor
Derek Rust offered his flock an anonymous way to redeem
themselves; he asked congregation members to drop off at the
church things they had stolen. Leading the way was the pastor
himself, who had borrowed some yard tools that he had never
returned. Church members, though, surpassed even Rust's
expectations. The pews overflowed with purloined items,
including a CD that belonged to the church, shirts, hotel towels, money, a power drill, a rubber toy eagle, and bubble gum
(unchewed).

Faster Than a Speeding Cycle

In September 2004, a State Patrol officer flying over Wabasha,
Minnesota, observed two motorcycles racing. When one surged
ahead, the officer hit his stopwatch and clicked it again when
the bike had gone a quarter mile. The time read 4.39 seconds,
or 205 mph, 140 mph over the speed limit. After the incident,
the officer said that the motorcycle had been going faster than
his plane! He contacted officers on the ground and warned

them of the oncoming speeder. When those officers caught up with the biker, he had slowed to 100 mph. The officers on the ground issued him a ticket, and although there is no official list, it is believed to be the "fastest speed" speeding ticket issued in Minnesota.

Caught with Their SquarePants Missing

In November 2004, a Minnesota Burger King was missing its blowup figure of SpongeBob SquarePants. The inflatable character had been displayed on the roof to promote an upcoming SpongeBob movie, but one night, he disappeared. Initially, police were hot on his scent and quickly discovered a ransom note demanding 10 crabby patties, fries, and milk shakes in exchange for SpongeBob's safe return. The nom de plume on the note was none other than Plankton, SpongeBob's archenemy. The pants-nappers also made threats; their missive stated that Patrick the Starfish would be next. They even committed crimes in other states; Wisconsin, Utah, Ohio, Virginia, and Michigan were all missing their SpongeBobs. Burger King offered a reward of a year's supply of Burger Bucks for information leading to SpongeBob's safe return. But police had few leads, and the Minnesota pants-nappers remain at large.

Throw Another Chip on the Fire

Ah, Minnesota, a state of invention and innovation: waterskiing, flour milling, and even an alternative energy solution. So what if it's turkey dung that's going to wean us off of foreign oil?

A poop power plant is currently under construction in Benson and slated to open in 2007. Why turkeys? Well, because their dung is dry, it burns cleaner and more easily than pig or cow chips. The Benson plant will be modeled after three already in operation in England and, once it gets going, will burn 700,000 tons of turkey droppings a year and supply power to more than 50,000 homes. So scoff if you must, but next Thanksgiving, remember that leftovers aren't just for eating anymore.

DID YOU KNOW?

In 1943, Minnesota's legislature asked the federal government to set up a prisoner-of-war camp in the state. Laborers in agriculture and other industries were leaving in droves to join the military and fight in World War II. The legislature reasoned that prisoners-of-war could fill the empty positions. The federal government agreed, and the first two camps opened in Olivia and Princeton in September 1943. Nineteen more camps followed, though most Minnesotans had no idea the camps existed. In all, 3,000 POWs were held in Minnesota between 1943 and the summer of 1945.

Axel and His Dog

*From 1954 to 1966, children in the Twin Cities fell in love
with a Scandinavian goof named Axel, his dog Towser,
and a cast of unique Minnesota characters.*

On the Radio

Axel was the creation of radio and television personality
Clellan Card, who was born in Minneapolis in 1903. Card grew
up to be an important part of Twin Cities' radio; during the
1930s and 1940s, he worked for each of the four major radio
broadcasting stations in the area.

Card's first radio job was in 1930. His father, a dentist, gave
a series of lectures on local station WCCO, and Card often
went to see his father speak. While there, Card also chatted
with radio personnel, and the station's staffers liked the sound
of his voice. That got Card an audition. A few weeks later, he
had his first on-air job, playing a fisherman on a program
sponsored by a rod and reel company. He also got his first "talent" check; Card made $4.50 for the spot.

Card quickly began to make a name for himself on Twin
Cities' radio. He worked his way up from bit spots to carry his
own show, *Almanac of the Air,* in 1936. Over the next two
decades, his career ebbed and flowed while he performed on
many comedy and children's radio programs for stations in

Minneapolis and Saint Paul. Then, in 1954, WCCO-TV offered him the opportunity to host a children's television program.

Welcome to the Tree House

The character of Axel had been part of Card's early radio shows but transferred easily to the small screen. Axel was Scandinavian (actually, he called himself "Scandihoovian"). He spoke with a Swedish accent and filled airtime with riddles, songs, puns, stories of his alma mater "Old Embraceable U," and general clowning around. One time, he even suggested on air that children should wake up their parents by throwing water in their faces (no one seems to know how many Twin Cities parents woke up wet the next day). Axel sported a thick moustache and wore a striped shirt, a conductor's hat, and green khaki pants held up by a rope; he also carried a magical telescope that he claimed let him see all the way to California. He had a dog named Towser, who was represented only by his paw; the dog's body was never seen. And the action took place in "Axel's tree house," where Axel and Towser lived.

The show, entitled *Axel and His Dog*, debuted on WCCO-TV on August 5, 1954, and it was an instant success. Axel became the top-rated afternoon program in the area, even beating out *American Bandstand*.

Soon, new characters joined Axel and Towser in the tree house. There was a cat named Tallulah who, like Towser, was a paws-only character. And there was Carmen the Nurse, played by dancer, singer, and Card radio show costar Mary Davies. *Axel and His Dog* also featured *Our Gang*, or *The Little Rascals*, shorts as part of the show.

The Birdie

Every episode ended the same way: with a takeoff of the Robert Louis Stevenson poem, *Time to Rise*. In his Scandihoovian accent, Axel recited the first three lines of the poem followed by a pun. For example, he might say,

Birdie with a yellow bill,
Hopped upon my windowsill,
Cocked a shining eye and says,
What was your boyfriend's name, Jesse, James?

Axel's version of the poem was called a "birdie," and the puns changed often. Some of them included the following:

What did you do when you sat on the bed, spring?
What did you do after you ate the ginger, snap?
What's the trouble with the baby, buggy?

Kids didn't always get the puns, but they enjoyed the silliness and the singsong cadence of Card's voice.

Carmen Delivers the Bad News

For 12 years, *Axel and His Dog* was a staple on Twin Cities' television. People who grew up during that time remember it well. One Minneapolis native wrote that "watching Axel as a boy counts among my fondest childhood memories." And another man says that Axel "beat any cartoon ever done on TV and was a dead heat with Superman."

None of the children watching, though, knew that the man who brought Axel to life was battling cancer. During much of the show's run, Card was ill, and in April 1966, he died. Mary Davies as Carmen the Nurse took to the airwaves the next day and told the audience that Axel had passed away. For many of the children watching, it was as though they'd lost a close friend.

A month later, WCCO set up a memorial fund to honor Card. All money would go to the University of Minnesota Pediatrics Hospital. Children across the Twin Cities gathered up nickels, dimes, and quarters and sent the money to the hospital. By the end of the summer, $5,600 had been raised, and half had been donated in small change.

Fun Fact:
Both Towser and Tallulah were played by Don Stolz, now the owner of the Old Log Theater, a dinner/resort theater located near Lake Minnetonka in Greenwood, Minnesota.

DID YOU KNOW?

Lefse is a spud-tacular Minnesota delicacy. To celebrate the potato pancake, Barnesville, Minnesota, holds an annual Potato Days Festival, where one of the most popular activities is a National Lefse Cookoff. Contestants have one hour to roll and fry their lefse. The winner earns $200 and, more importantly, the title of America's Best Lefse Cook.

Name That Town!

Minnesotans have come up with a variety of names for the places they live—some sweet, some weird, and some completely baffling. Here are some of the oddest names to grace Minnesota towns, past and present, and how they came to be.

Balaton

Supposedly named after the western Hungarian Lake Balaton, but legends abound to explain the true origin. Some claim the town's name was inspired by its first merchant, David Bell (Bell-town changing to Balaton); others name a railroad stockholder named Balaton. And the most unique explanation is that local officials, at a loss for a name, decided to let the people vote for one: It required a "ballot-on."

Bogus Brook

A reference to counterfeit money and also the name of a nearby river. Why the lumberjacks who founded the town gave it or the river such a shady name, no one knows for sure.

Bungo

Named for the descendants of the African American slave Jean Bonga. They intermarried with Ojibwa Indians, altered the family name slightly to "Bungo," and served as interpreters for governors and generals.

Chanhassen

Founder Reverend Henry M. Nichols wanted his town's name to mean "sugar maple" in the language of the Dakota. Literally *chanhassen* is a compound Dakota word meaning the "tree of sweet juice," or the sugar maple.

Corvuso

A bastardization of the Latin word *corvus*, which means "crow." The area must have had a lot of them.

Darfur

A celebration of immigrant accents. Supposedly, Scandinavian railroad men in the area would ask, "Why you stop dar fur?"

Dentaybow

A combination of three local farmers' names: Densmore, Taylor, and Bowman.

Lucan

Officially named for a town in Ireland, but local legend offers a more interesting explanation. The story goes that when a railroad surveyor was asked if he could come up with a name for the town, he answered, "No, but maybe Lou can," making a reference to his coworker, Lou Kartak.

Money Creek

The town was christened after a local creek that, in turn, can thank a clumsy man for its name. The fellow had gotten his wallet wet in the creek and was drying its contents on a shrub when a gust of wind blew his money back into the water, and some of it was lost forever.

Moonshine

The town was named after a nearby lake. In 1876, after setting up camp on the shore, David Clark decided to christen it "Moon Lake" after his wife, Mary Moon. But that night, as he watched the moon rise and its light reflect off the water, he made a slight change.

Nodine

Two surveyors came here and couldn't find a single place to eat.

Pease

There was a railroad man by the name of Granville S. Pease associated with the town, but local legend says that the name is simply a typographical mistake; the town's residents wanted to name it "Peace."

Quiring

A meeting called to choose a name for this town became a bit rowdy, and one of the organizers urged the crowd to "be quiet and stop quarreling." Instead of continuing to argue, the townsfolk did as they were told and then decided to combine the words "quiet" and "quarreling" to come up with the name for their town.

Honorable Mentions:

Some historical town names need no explanation.

These Sound Inviting

City of Attraction, Comfort, Dad's Corner, Eden, Home, Ideal, Lucknow, Nirvana, Rest Island, Welcome, Winner

These, Not so Much

Kiester, Leech, Lonesome, Looneyville, Mantrap, Nimrod, Pig's Eye, Pillager, Plugtown, Podunk, Pork Bay, Ransom, Rat Root, Red Eye, Savage, Strung Out Town, Swastika Beach

They Must Go to Church

Baptism, Conception, Faith, Lent

Ideal Towns

Choice, Equality, Excel, Freedom, Friendship, Harmony, Hope, Independence, Liberty, Peace, Progress, Prosper, Triumph, Victory

Animal Friendly

Badger, Buffalo, Bull Moose, Cormorant, Eagle Lake, Elk River, Fox, Hornet, Partridge, Wolf

Love Their Food

Blueberry, Cherry, Cream, Fruitville, Lime, Orange, Rice

International

Athens, Belgium, Berlin, Bombay, Cuba, Dublin, Oslo, Sweden, Warsaw

The Happy Warrior

His name graces the Metrodome, a terminal at the Minneapolis–Saint Paul airport, the public affairs building at the University of Minnesota, even the job corps in Saint Paul. But who was Hubert Humphrey, and why is he so important to Minnesota?

Hubert Horatio Humphrey Jr. was born in Wallace, South Dakota, on May 27, 1911. The Humphrey family, which included four children, soon moved to Doland, South Dakota, a small farming town of about 600. Hubert spent his early years there before heading east in 1929 to attend the University of Minnesota. Times were hard, though, and Hubert left school to return home and work at his father's drugstore. Still, he set his sights on finishing his studies. In the fall of 1937, with his family's blessing and $675 that he and his wife had saved together, the couple moved to Minneapolis.

Helloooooooooo Minnesota!

After graduation, Humphrey tried (and failed) to find work at the university. He took a job with the Works Progress Administration (WPA) instead. The WPA was a New Deal program that put skilled people to work on various government projects. Humphrey became director of the Twin City Workers Education program. Soon he was the program's state director. By the spring of 1943, Humphrey had amassed a local network of supporters and political contacts around Minneapolis, and he decided the time had come to run for political office. It was a quick decision. Only 19 days before the May 10 mayoral primary, Humphrey quit his government job and filed his Democratic candidacy for mayor of Minneapolis.

Of the eight candidates, several were better known than Humphrey. But he wasn't going to let that stop him. He raced around Minneapolis, addressing every neighborhood club that would listen. But it wasn't his time. The Humphrey campaign, although dynamic (a trait he'd become known for), was also disorganized (another trademark) and ineffective. He lost that first election.

Going Like Gangbusters

The loss was a disappointment but not a defeat. Humphrey continued to rise in Minneapolis politics. He played a key role in the merging of the Democratic and Farmer-Labor parties (the latter was a powerful leftist coalition that had held the balance of power in Minnesota politics for decades) and then ran for mayor again in 1945 on a platform of law and order. He promised to drive the gangsters and racketeers out of Minneapolis and to choose a tough police chief to clean up the city. He also received endorsements from the AFL (American Federation of Labor), CIO (Congress of Industrial Organizations), and railway unions. In the 1940s, Minneapolis was a union town, and the endorsements helped. This time, he won.

True to his word, Humphrey dedicated himself to reducing organized crime. He appointed a burly Irishman named Ed

Ryan as chief of police, and together, the two gained the upper hand against organized crime. One story tells of Humphrey meeting with Minneapolis crime boss Chickie Berman. Humphrey told his constituents that his door was always open, so when Berman requested a meeting, the mayor obliged. What Berman wanted, though, was to buy Humphrey's support of his crime syndicate, and he offered up 25 percent of his business profits. Humphrey responded by saying his price was 75 percent. "My god," Berman exclaimed. "That would break us." To which Humphrey responded, "That's exactly right—and that's what's going to happen to you."

Humphrey often called his time as mayor of Minneapolis the best job he'd ever had. He rode with the cops on their night patrols. He visited the scenes of fires. He read the comics over the radio to children during the 1946 polio epidemic. By the time his 1947 reelection came around, he was a shoo-in. Humphrey rolled over his opponent by a 50,000-vote margin, a record in Minneapolis city elections.

To the Senate

But Hubert Humphrey was ambitious and already looking beyond state politics. He wanted to win the U.S. Senate seat held by Republican Joseph Ball.

Ball and Humphrey met only once, for a radio debate staged by the League of Women Voters. It wasn't much of a contest. Humphrey outspoke and outperformed his rival. Effervescent and hyperenergized but always on task, he was dubbed the "happy warrior" of Minnesota politics.

And he took that show on the road. Throughout 1948, he

visited each of Minnesota's 87 counties at least once. He attended almost every county fair and hand-shook and baby-kissed his way through festivals galore: the Sauerkraut Festival at Springfield, Watermelon Day at Sanborn, Turkey Day at Worthington, the Bohemian Dance at Owatonna, and the Finnish Society at Duluth. In all, he made about 700 speeches and traveled 31,000 miles. Meanwhile, virtually every major American union sent money and manpower into Minnesota to help Humphrey beat Ball. And beat Ball he did. Humphrey carried 85 out of 87 counties.

Jousting the King of Camelot

Humphrey triumphed again in 1954 when he won reelection to the Senate by 162,000 votes. His home base secure, he turned his attention to the national stage. Hubert Humphrey wanted to be president.

The problem was that in 1960, the year Humphrey tried for his first Democratic presidential nomination, another young, dynamic man was on the ticket: John F. Kennedy. Kennedy had charm, charisma, and money Humphrey couldn't match. Like he'd done in his quests for mayor and senator, Humphrey took his campaign to the people. He campaigned hard in the early Wisconsin and West Virginia primaries, shaking hands and giving roadside speeches. But he was no match for the Kennedy political machine. Kennedy pamphlets and bumper stickers deluged both states, and Kennedy ads saturated the newspapers, TV, and radio. It was an organized, well-oiled effort that, in the end, simply defeated the Humphrey team. Humphrey lost both states.

Some (Gentle) Whipping of His Own

The primary defeats were tough to take, but Humphrey turned around and won reelection to the Senate by nearly a quarter of a million votes. This lifted him out of the political ashes and into the most satisfying and productive period of his life. He became the majority whip of the Senate. He also built an impressive record of achievement in Congress, with such landmark accomplishments as passage of legislation supporting the Peace Corps, the Occupational Safety and Health Act (OSHA), and the Nuclear Test Ban Treaty between the United States and the Soviet Union. But it was the passage in the Senate of the Civil Rights Act of 1964 that Humphrey called "my greatest achievement."

A Nation in Turmoil

In November 1963, Kennedy was assassinated, and Lyndon B. Johnson took over the presidency, leaving the office of the vice president open. When the Democratic convention rolled around the following year, Johnson chose Hubert Humphrey as his running mate.

On January 20, 1965, Humphrey took the oath as the 38th Vice President of the United States. Humphrey had paid his dues, but Johnson proved unwilling to share the spotlight with his vice president. Hubert Humphrey had no choice but to defer to the president on all issues. One of the issues on which the two men disagreed was Vietnam.

The 1968 presidential election was a doozy. Johnson, faced with tremendous unpopularity because of his decision to keep America involved in the Vietnam War, announced that he would not run for reelection. Hugely popular liberal candidate Robert Kennedy made eyes at the Democratic nomination but was assassinated in June 1968. With the frontrunner gone, Humphrey became the Democrats' presidential nominee.

His years in the unpopular Johnson White House proved to be his downfall. No amount of campaigning could erase Vietnam from the American memory, and Humphrey refused to speak out against Johnson's Vietnam policy. His Republican foe in the 1968 election was Richard Nixon, a man who had no trouble disagreeing with Johnson and who promised to get America out of Vietnam. In the end, Humphrey lost, but the election was close; the popular vote went to Nixon by less than 1 percent.

The Golden Years

The 1968 defeat was hard for Humphrey, but in true "happy warrior" fashion, he picked up and moved on. In 1969, he took a job teaching at Macalester College in Saint Paul and, in 1970, was reelected to the Senate. There he continued to work until his death in January 1978.

DID YOU KNOW?

The total distance of all groomed snowmobile trails in Minnesota is 12,000 miles, more than any other U.S. state.

Grace: The State Photograph

In 1918, when Charles Wilden showed up at Eric Enstrom's
photography studio in Bovey, a small mining community in northern
Minnesota, Wilden was just hoping to make a sale. A peddler by trade,
Wilden stopped by Enstrom's place intending to sell the photographer
some boot scrapers. Enstrom had other ideas.

Getting the Shot

On seeing Wilden, Enstrom thought, "There was something
about the old gentleman's face that immediately impressed me.
I saw that he had a kind face . . . There weren't any harsh lines
in it." It was a face, Enstrom believed, that needed to be in
pictures.

So Enstrom convinced the elderly gentleman to pose for a
photograph. On a small table, Enstrom placed a book, a bowl
of gruel, a loaf of bread, a knife, and a pair of glasses. He asked
Wilden to sit down, bow his head, and fold his hands against
his forehead. This modest picture, a man in prayer before his
meal, became known as *Grace.*

International *Grace*

It was a simple photograph for a not-so-simple time. In 1918,
World War I had just ended in Europe, but for four years, it

had ravaged the continent and exhausted much of the Western world. Enstrom said, "I wanted to take a picture that would show people that even though they had to do without many things because of the war they still had much to be thankful for." He succeeded. People traveling through Bovey were so taken with the photo hanging in Enstrom's studio that he found himself churning out print after print for anxious buyers.

Over the next quarter century, the basic premise of the photo stayed the same, but it was sometimes customized. Enstrom used photographic oils, paints specialized for use on prints, to colorize the photo. If a customer preferred that Wilden be wearing a green shirt, for instance, Enstrom painted the shirt green. In the 1930s, Enstrom's daughter Rhoda, a painter by trade, took over the job. The colorized prints often made *Grace* look more like an oil painting than a photograph.

In 1945, 70 years old and unable to keep up with the demand for his print, Enstrom sold *Grace's* copyright to the Augsberg Publishing House in Minneapolis (though he maintained royalty rights). That company mass-produced the photograph, and since then, millions of copies have made their way around the world.

It's Official

In 2002, the Minnesota legislature recognized *Grace* as the state's official photograph. There was some initial criticism of a picture that seemed to promote religious themes taking on that status. In fact, a Grand Rapids businessman named C. C. Peterson had written a prayer to go with the photo. But, said

State Representative Bob Lessard, who lobbied for the photo to be adopted officially, "That's not what it's about. This picture, I think, represents an elderly person showing his emotions, showing how he feels."

DID YOU KNOW?

The Anderson Center, an artists' community in Red Wing, was once the home of Alexander Pierce Anderson, the inventor of puffed rice cereal. When A. P. Anderson and his family lived there, the 330-acre property was called the Tower View Complex and was a working farm, laboratory, and home. It also included a 25,000-gallon water tower that Anderson had constructed to provide running water to the complex. A room at the very top served as his laboratory. In 1995, A. P. Anderson's grandson, Robert Hedin, turned the property into an artists' colony, where writers, painters, sculptors, and others from around the world come to study and work. The organization also puts on community art shows and presentations. To date, the Anderson Center has hosted more than 300 artists-in-residence from 20 countries and more than 16,000 tourists. The Anderson Center is the largest artists' community in Minnesota.

Flour Power: Milling in Minneapolis

In the beginning, there was General Mills.

In 1856, a man with the impressive name of Cadwallader C. "C. C." Washburn bought a section of land along the Mississippi River. His section also included Saint Anthony Falls, a landmark revered by Native Americans and considered a valuable energy source by pioneers. Washburn formed a company called the Minneapolis Milling Company and leased the energy rights along that section of the Mississippi to flour and lumber millers.

Getting to Know Washburn

C. C. Washburn is credited with making Minneapolis a flour milling center, but he never actually lived in Minnesota. Born in Livermore, Maine, Washburn first became a teacher in that state. At 21, he decided to go west. He eventually became a lawyer and settled in Mineral Point, Wisconsin.

There he remained and played a prominent role in politics. From 1854 to 1861, he served as a Republican Representative in the U.S. Congress. When the Civil War broke out, he joined the Union army, rose to the rank of major general, and led a cavalry division at the Battle of Vicksburg. After the war, Washburn returned to Wisconsin and served as that state's governor from 1872 to 1874. He died in 1882.

Washburn's Folly

During his life, Washburn was a shrewd investor, and he saw Saint Anthony Falls as an opportunity. As a lessor of power rights to the Minnesota milling industry, Washburn was perfectly situated to recognize a good opportunity when he saw it. In 1866, 10 years after founding the Minneapolis Milling Company, he built his own flour mill near the falls. It was called the "Washburn B-Mill." Six stories tall, it was the largest mill west of Rochester, New York (a major East Coast flour-milling town), and cost $100,000 to construct. Locals thought Washburn had lost his mind, that there would never be enough demand for Midwestern wheat flour to warrant such a huge expenditure of money. Midwestern flour was considered by many to be inferior—too coarse and dark for mainstream consumption. Midwestern farmers also had trouble getting their wheat seeds to survive the region's harsh winters; thus, crops were unreliable. As such, locals dubbed the mill "Washburn's Folly" and were sure it would go bust.

The naysayers were wrong. As new strains of wheat called "spring wheat" were developed to withstand the winter, flour from the Midwest became increasingly popular. Things went so well, in fact, that in 1874, Washburn opened a second, larger mill in the area. It was called the "Washburn A-Mill." Traditionally, the letter designation in mills' names has nothing to do with the order in which they open, but everything to do with their size; an A-Mill is larger than a B-Mill.

Washburn's mills were so prosperous that, in 1877, he took two partners—his brother and a man named John Crosby. The newly formed partnership led to a new name for the company: the Washburn Crosby Company.

From Tragedy Comes Innovation

Flour milling, however, can be dangerous work. The atmosphere inside a mill, where flour dust mixes with oxygen, is highly combustible. Any spark, perhaps caused by overheating machinery, can lead to an explosion. On May 2, 1878, this happened at the Washburn A-Mill. It exploded, killing 14 employees.

Washburn immediately set about rebuilding the mill. During rebuilding, he included a number of innovations that improved mill safety and modernized the industry. In particular, he introduced the use of automatic steel rollers instead of the grinding stones typically used. This innovation made his mill the first automatic roller mill in the world, and it allowed Washburn to create a new and improved type of flour. The new flour was whiter and finer than any other, and it was about to make Washburn (well, his flour at least) a household name.

Medals? We've Got Medals!

In 1880, the Washburn Crosby Company entered the new flour in a competition at the International Millers' Exhibition in Cincinnati, Ohio. There was nothing else like it, and Washburn Crosby took home three medals: gold, silver, and bronze. In commemoration, Washburn and his partners named their winning flour Gold Medal flour.

The brand became extremely popular. Bakers around the country chose Gold Medal flour, recognizing it immediately by its white bag with distinctive orange and blue markings. Today, it remains the world's most popular and recognizable brand of flour.

Birth of a Conglomerate

In 1928, the Washburn Crosby Company merged with several other U.S. mills. The new company was named General Mills, and within five months, it was the largest flour miller in the world.

A year later, the American stock market crashed and plunged the country into the Great Depression. As many businesses took hit after hit, General Mills remained strong. Economical and comforting, home baking skyrocketed during those troubled times. As Americans consumed more and more flour (especially Gold Medal flour), General Mills' stock took off.

Ready for War

Although its flour remains popular, over the years, General Mills has gotten involved in creating all kinds of new products. All the machinery involved in the milling process was complicated, and rather than outsource all the building and repair, General Mills started an engineering division to keep things running smoothly. From there, using the company's engineering resources for other purposes was easy.

During the 1940s, General Mills participated in research and development for the U.S. military. The products it developed included torpedoes, gun sights, and other precision instruments with military applications. One weapon in particular, named the hedgehog, guided missiles to their targets and helped to sink 300 German submarines. General Mills engineers also worked on improved naval gun sights that were used during the battle of Iwo Jima.

Making a Mark on the Media

Throughout the 1920s, 1930s, 1940s, and 1950s, General Mills hit the airwaves. In 1924, the company bought the radio station WCCO (the call letters stand for Washburn Crosby Company) and entered the entertainment business to diversify its business holdings and promote its products. Shows like *Gold Medal Flour Home Service Talks* and the *Betty Crocker Cooking School of the Air* made their way to American homes daily. CBS bought WCCO in 1932, but General Mills continued to be a part of the programming; Wheaties, a General Mills product, sponsored the first children's adventure series on radio, called *Jack Armstrong, the All-American Boy*. In all, General Mills backed more than 200 radio programs through the mid-1950s.

Maintaining its innovative streak, General Mills also got involved in television. The first televised sporting event, a baseball game between the Brooklyn Dodgers and the Cincinnati Reds, was a General Mills–sponsored event. And as television overtook radio in popularity, General Mills went right along. From *The Lone Ranger* to *I Love Lucy* to *The Ed Sullivan Show*, General Mills sponsored some of the most popular programs on TV.

Today, General Mills remains one of the strongest and most profitable companies in the United States. It owns many of the food brands we use every day, including Cheerios, Wheaties, Bisquick, Chex, Total, Trix, Cocoa Puffs, Hamburger Helper, Progresso soups, Fruit Roll-Ups, Pop Secret popcorn, and Yoplait yogurt. General Mills has also merged with some of America's most well-known companies, including Pillsbury and Green Giant.

For the Pillsbury part of the story, turn to page 223.
To read about General Mills advertising icons, turn to page 266.

DID YOU KNOW?

The 45th parallel, the halfway point between the equator and the north pole, runs right through the yard of Golden Valley, Minnesota, residents Javetta and Amando Dickerson. There's even a rock and plaque to mark the spot, though the Dickersons were unaware of the rock's importance until early 2006. After much time spent wondering why so many cars slowed down to look at the rock (some people even stopped to sit on it and have their picture taken!), the Dickersons investigated and discovered the plaque. Today, they welcome curious visitors but ask that anyone stopping by do so courteously and not bother the house.

Good Grief!

*Born in Minneapolis and raised in Saint Paul, Charles Schulz
created some of the most enduring characters of all time. His Peanuts
cartoons and the children who inhabit them (led by the oft-abused
Charlie Brown) have been making us laugh since they debuted in
1950. Here's a look at Schulz and Peanuts by the numbers.*

0

Laugh tracks used on Charlie Brown TV specials. Schulz insisted
that viewers should be able to enjoy the cartoons and not be told
when to laugh. CBS network executives did create a version of *A
Charlie Brown Christmas* with a laugh track in case Schulz came
around to their way of thinking, but it was never used.

1

Number of times Lucy actually let Charlie Brown kick the football. This comic appeared in the early 1990s.

3rd

Grade that Charlie Brown has attended since he first appeared
in newsprint in 1950

5¢

Amount Lucy charges for counseling services. The first advice
she gave to Charlie Brown was "Get over it!"

10

The Apollo mission number that had modules named for Charlie Brown (the command module) and Snoopy (the lunar module)

$90

Amount Charles Schulz made for his first month of *Peanuts* cartoon strips in October 1950

930

Number of games Charlie Brown's baseball team lost over the years; they've won two.

1947

The year Schulz sold his first regular cartoon strip to the *Saint Paul Pioneer Press*. The series was called *Li'l Folks*, and it ran until 1949. There are some similarities between this strip and the *Peanuts* series: a dog in *Li'l Folks* resembles Snoopy, there's a character named Charlie Brown, and there's a well-dressed boy who loves Beethoven and playing the piano (like Schroeder in *Peanuts*).

1968

The year Franklin, an African American character, joined the *Peanuts* gang. Charles Schulz always said that he introduced Franklin only as a new character, not as a political statement. But arriving as he did during the Civil Rights era and sitting next to Charlie Brown in school, Franklin inspired a lot of talk (and some backlash) about integration.

2,400

Number of newspapers that include Schulz's *Peanuts* cartoons today. These are all old comics; the last new strip ran on January 3, 2000, a month before Schulz died.

$35 million+

Amount Charles Schulz made (and his estate continues to make) from *Peanuts*

Fun Facts:

- Charles Schulz once had a real-life friend named Charlie Brown and a crush on a "little red-haired girl" named Donna Johnson.
- Schulz never liked the name *Peanuts*. United Feature Syndicate, the syndication service that bought the cartoons in 1950, chose the name. Schulz felt *Peanuts* was confusing and silly because it had nothing to do with the cartoons' themes or subject matter. Instead, he wanted to call the comic *Good Ol' Charlie Brown*.

DID YOU KNOW?

Minnesota is home to one of America's landmark freedom of speech cases. In 1931, the U.S. Supreme Court ruled that Minneapolis news-paperman Jay Near had the right to print accusations about public figures as long as he could present evidence supporting them. The decision continues to protect publishers of newspapers, magazines, and other periodicals from legal retaliation by the subjects of their exposés.

The Missing Link

During the late 1960s, Minnesotans went ape for a
Sasquatch-like creature known as the Minnesota Iceman.

The year was 1968. Enter Minnesota's Frank Hansen. Sensing an opportunity to exploit the public's fascination with the wild and the weird, the veteran carny began touring local fairs with a new attraction, something he called the "Famous Missing Link Iceman." For 35 cents, carnival goers could enter Hansen's mobile refrigeration unit and glimpse the Iceman, a hairy, six-foot tall beast embedded in a block of thick ice. Adding to the creature's mystery was the fact that it appeared to have been shot in the eye.

The Legend

According to Hansen, the creature had been discovered by fishermen who found it entombed in nearly three tons of ice off the coast of Siberia. Intrigued by their discovery, the fishermen brought it onboard their ship and later sold it to an emporium in Hong Kong where it caught the eye of an anonymous American oil tycoon. The tycoon bought it and then chose to rent the creature to Hansen so it could become a traveling sideshow attraction.

The Iceman might have remained a quaint, local attraction had two cryptozoologists (people who study legendary creatures like bigfoot) not caught wind of it. In December 1968, Ivan T. Sanderson and Bernard Heuvelmans read a magazine story about the Iceman and came to Hansen's home in Rollingstone, Minnesota, to inspect the creature. Although Hansen wouldn't let the men remove the Iceman from his tomb, the pair conducted what they called "a thorough examination" and were both astonished by what they found. Noting an "appalling stench of rotting flesh," Sanderson and Heuvelmans declared that the Iceman was genuine and called him "the fresh remains of a Neanderthaloid human."

On Thin Ice

Hansen pleaded with the men to keep their findings to themselves, but they passed their notes on to magazine publishers. As the Iceman's story spread, the Smithsonian Institute got involved and, in March 1969, requested permission to x-ray the creature. Hansen refused, claiming that the Iceman had been repossessed by its millionaire owner and would never be shown to the public again. When the FBI began investigating the creature's origin and cause of death, Hansen disappeared. One month later, on April 21, 1969, he gave a press conference where he revealed what he called a replica of the Iceman and announced that he'd now be touring the country with that.

This odd behavior and suspicion about the Iceman's origins ruined Hansen's credibility and led Sanderson and Heuvelmans to retract their earlier claims. Sanderson even went so far as to investigate Hansen himself and discovered that as early as 1967, the carny had hired Hollywood special effects companies to construct several latex Icemen.

For his part, Hansen never denied having the replicas made but said he used them only after the initial barrage of publicity in 1969, when he returned the Iceman to its still-unnamed owner. He also never retracted his claim of the creature's origin and, as of 1995, said he didn't even know the truth himself. "I never did find out," he said when asked about the Iceman's authenticity. "I just knew, whatever it was, it was just the greatest exhibit possible."

DID YOU KNOW?

The first patient treated successfully for pulmonary tuberculosis (also called TB or consumption) was an Austin, Minnesota, woman named Patricia. She was hospitalized at the Mineral Springs Sanatorium in Cannon Falls and then at the Mayo Clinic in Rochester. Patricia received injections of an experimental antibiotic called streptomycin from November 20, 1944, to April 7, 1945. The treatment saved her life and proved that doctors had finally found a cure for the once-believed incurable deadly disease.

What a Turkey!

Worthington, Minnesota, considered itself the undisputed "Turkey Capital of the World," until turkey-crazed Cuero, Texas, found out.

In September 1939, Worthington residents threw their first King Turkey Day Festival to celebrate the town's thriving turkey industry. It was a low-key but well-attended affair. Politicians and journalists flocked to the celebration. Downtown merchants dressed up as farmers and attended the free pancake breakfast and parade. And revelers collected souvenir turkey feathers from large barrels on Main Street.

The next year, Minnesota's governor gave the festival's keynote address, and *Life* magazine captured the event on film. King Turkey Day quickly became an annual event, and Worthingtonians proudly proclaimed their town the "Turkey Capital of the World."

The Turkey Trot

It turns out that Cuero, Texas, is equally proud of its turkey history. Cuero has been turning out turkeys since 1908, and in 1920, the Turkey Trot Festival (now called Turkeyfest) was born.

Residents felt confident that their turkey celebration was unrivaled in America. But in 1972, they learned the painful truth: Worthington also claimed a right to the turkey throne.

North Vs. South

Which town first challenged the other remains unclear. But what's certain is that both towns quickly agreed the only way to officially determine who was the true Turkey Capital of the World was to have it out in an annual turkey race.

The race has two legs. The first run takes place during Worthington's King Turkey Day (the second Saturday after Labor Day) and the second as part of Turkeyfest (the second weekend in October); the combined race times yield an overall champion. Worthington's entry is always named Paycheck, since "nothing goes faster than a paycheck," and Ruby Begonia hails from Cuero. The rules are tough and clear; handlers cannot touch their birds once the race begins, and time penalties are assessed for infractions or if a turkey escapes the track.

Sometimes, the race ends in a photo finish. The closest margin of victory was a nine-tenths of a second win by Paycheck in 1977. More often, though, there's an obvious winner. Worthington has taken more titles (17) than Cuero (15). And to the winner go the spoils: the "Traveling Turkey Trophy of Tumultuous Triumph." The loser goes home with the "Circulating Cup of Consummate Commiseration."

The competition doesn't end on the racetrack. Each town also tries to outdo the other in the festivities surrounding the race. Cuerovians boast activities such as turkey bowling (tossing frozen turkeys at pins), cow-patty bingo, and a parade with the (sometimes) victorious Ruby riding a float. Worthingtonians answer with, among other things, jugglers, an antique tractor show, and, of course, the pancake breakfast. No matter who wins, both of these towns sure love their turkeys.

A Trip Down the Mighty Mississip'

*From its source in northern Minnesota, the Mississippi River
begins a journey to the Gulf of Mexico. As the river meanders more
than 600 miles through Minnesota, it passes lakes, small towns,
and big cities. Here are five historic stops along the way.*

Veritas Caput

Back in the early 1800s, a lot of European explorers wanted to
find the source of the Mississippi River. The Native Americans
already knew where it was, so it's not surprising that it was an
Indian guide who led European Henry Rowe Schoolcraft to
Lake Itasca, the source of the mighty river. According to most
history books, Schoolcraft thought "Elk," the Native American
name for the lake, not quite up to snuff. So he took syllables
from the Latin words *verITAS CAput,* which means true head,
and created the word "Itasca."

The 1.7-square-mile Lake Itasca now sits in the oldest state
park in Minnesota. Here, the Mississippi river is only 20 to 30
feet wide (its narrowest span) and three feet deep. Since Itasca
State Park was established in 1891, thousands of visitors have
come to see the river's source and to cross its humble beginnings on a series of sometimes slippery stepping-stones.

There's No Place Like Home

Downriver, near a spot where the Mississippi falls about five feet in a third of a mile, is Grand Rapids, the birthplace of Frances Gumm. Frances, better known as Judy Garland, left town in 1926, but there's no place like the Grand Rapids home where she lived for the first four years of her life. The house has been moved from its original site twice (in 1938 and 1994). The most recent move occurred so it could be renovated as part of the Judy Garland Museum next door. Memorabilia inside the museum include the *Wizard of Oz* carriage, an "Over the Rainbow" gold record, and a microphone from Judy Garland's TV show. Plus, every June since 1975, Grand Rapids has hosted the Judy Garland Festival, an event that has brought countless visitors to the city, including actor Mickey Rooney, Judy Garland's three children, and many of the original Munchkins.

Lindbergh's Little Falls

From Grand Rapids, the Mississippi meanders southward to Little Falls. There, along the shore of the river, is Lindbergh State Park. Although the park is named for early-1900s Minnesota congressman Charles Lindbergh Sr., it was the congressman's son, Charles Jr., who brought worldwide attention to the family's hometown. In 1927, Junior (a.k.a. Lucky Lindy) became the first person to fly solo across the Atlantic Ocean. A full-scale replica of the cockpit of the *Spirit of Saint Louis,* the plane he took on that historic flight, is on display at the park's visitor center, and the restored family home is open to the public.

Snelling's Fort

Not far from Lindbergh Park, the Mississippi meets up with the Minnesota River. A sacred site to Native Americans, the spot is also home to the first European settlement in the area. During the early 1820s, Colonel Josiah Snelling guided the construction of a military outpost. The fort played host to trading and talks between settlers and the Dakota and Ojibwa tribes. In the early 1850s, as westward expansion continued, the fort became a supply depot. Later, the area was sold and set to become a town site, but those plans were scrapped when the Civil War began and the fort was called into action as a training center for Union troops.

The U.S. military continued to use the fort until it closed just after World War II. Then, in the 1950s, urban development threatened the historic site, and Minnesotans worked to save Fort Snelling. It became a National Historic Landmark in 1960 and has since been restored to replicate an 1820s military outpost.

Samuelson Skis

South of Fort Snelling, where the Mississippi defines the border between Minnesota and Wisconsin, is the town of Lake City. Along the town's eastern shore, there is a wide spot in the river known as Lake Pepin. It was on Lake Pepin in 1922 that an 18-year-old Lake City resident named Ralph Samuelson invented the sport of waterskiing. Samuelson thought up waterskiing while sliding down snow-covered hills in the winter. He could ski on snow, why not on water? He first tried to translate snow skiing to waterskiing by using barrel staves and snow skis to glide over the water. That didn't work; the skis sank into the water, and he always fell. Five days later, he tried again with skis shaped out of tow board. He boiled the skis' tips, curved them up, and then tried them out. Also, instead of leaning forward, he leaned back on the skis and discovered he could skim across the surface while his brother towed him behind their boat. Success!

DID YOU KNOW?

After he retired, Charles Mayo bought a 3,000-acre farm on the outskirts of Rochester and named it Mayowood. There he began a new career as a dairy farmer. Charlie was Rochester's public health officer at the time, and he wanted to make sure the town had a supply of good, safe, pasteurized milk. Local dairymen thought pasteurization was unnecessary and too expensive to implement. So Charlie did it himself, making Mayowood one of Minnesota's most successful dairy farms.

Dayton's: Right on Target

*A Minneapolis staple, the Dayton Corporation became
the Target Corporation and was the force behind one of the
most recognizable retail chains in the United States.*

In 1883, New Englander George Draper Dayton arrived in
Worthington, Minnesota. He was an entrepreneur, looking for
opportunity in the newly settled Midwest, and over the next 15
years, Dayton and his family became a fixture in town. He built
a magnificent home on the prairie, took over Worthington's
failing bank, and became an advocate for building homes and
communities. But the prairie town was too small for Dayton's
ambition. He wanted to get involved in business, so he scouted
cities like Chicago and Saint Louis, looking for a place that
offered the right balance of consumers and opportunity. In the
end, he found what he was looking for in the young city of
Minneapolis.

At the turn of the 20th century, Minneapolis was a city on
the rise. Believing that much of the city's future rested in retail
and that the part of town just waiting to boom was at the corner of 7th Street and Nicollet Avenue, Dayton began buying
property in the area and convincing retailers to become his ten-
ants. A local department store moved into Dayton's building at
7th and Nicollet, but the store soon failed; competition in the

area was just too fierce. Rather than admit defeat, Dayton bought the store. He and his son turned it into a dry goods store, and by 1902, Dayton's was a force to be reckoned with.

Generous George

The Dayton Dry Goods Company (later, just the Dayton Company) grew quickly. Within a few years, it comprised an entire city block along Nicollet Avenue. Dayton ran his store the way he lived his life: respectfully and with a personal touch. He valued his employees and personally handed out candy to them every Christmas Eve. He admired timeliness and was known to lock latecomers out of meetings. He insisted that no alcohol be sold in his store and forbade employees from conducting any business, including advertising, on Sunday.

Dayton also wanted to share his good fortune. In 1918, he established the Dayton Foundation, a philanthropic organization that contributed to local communities. To get the foundation going, Dayton endowed it with $1 million. In 1946, generosity became company creed when the Dayton Company promised to return 5 percent of pretax profits from its stores to the communities in which they operated.

Class and Southdale

After George Dayton's death in 1938, his sons and grandsons took charge of the company. Nelson Dayton ran his father's business until 1950, when he passed away and the third generation of Daytons (Nelson's five sons) took over. Many things changed during this period. The bans on liquor sales and Sunday business were history. And high class came to

Minnesota by way of Dayton's. The store held annual spring flower shows and created elaborate window displays at Christmas. Women could buy their clothes in perfumed salons reminiscent of Europe's design houses. Valets loaded cars while patrons shopped. And on its shopping bags, Dayton's showcased the work of local artists.

In 1956, the Dayton Company opened Southdale, the first indoor shopping mall, in the Minneapolis suburb of Edina. Initially, the mall was envisioned as an entire community complete with shopping, apartments, parks, and more, and the Daytons invested $20 million in the project. In the end, finances dictated that only the shopping mall was constructed, but it proved tremendously popular. There were 72 stores, including two competing department stores; Southdale was the first shopping center to house competitors in the same building. Parking was free, and the mall's 5,000 parking spaces were organized into lots that used symbols to clearly identify each lot. This made it easier for patrons to find their cars after a day of shopping. Southdale's design made it a focal point of the community and the model for the many suburban shopping malls that followed. The shopping center also offered an interesting amenity not duplicated at later malls: a helicopter flew shoppers from Southdale to Dayton's store in Minneapolis, the airport, or downtown Saint Paul; the flying time was 10 minutes.

Bull's-eye!

The Daytons were on a roll. But by far, their greatest accomplishment and contribution to American retail came just a few years later. In the early 1960s, America was well into its population shift. Families were leaving urban areas and settling in suburbs where freeways and shopping malls made getting around and getting what one needed easy and convenient. The Dayton Company saw opportunity there. If the suburban housewife enjoyed the shopping mall, wouldn't she also like a discount department store?

The first Target store (complete with an early version of the now well-known bull's-eye logo) opened in Roseville, Minnesota, in 1962. It offered name-brand products at discounted prices. Better yet, everything was under one roof. There was no more schlepping from store to store for shampoo and socks and peanut butter. The busy housewife (who became and remains Target's primary customer) could get in and out quickly, find what she needed, and save a little money in the process.

Over the next few years, as more Target stores opened, they were all arranged according to similar blueprints. This made every location easy to navigate and recognizable to consumers. The stores were clean, well lit, and well organized. Shoppers flocked to Target, and by 1979, Target had become the Daytons' biggest moneymaker.

Bigger and Better

Never a family to rest on its laurels, the Daytons continued creating new opportunities. They founded many businesses during the mid-1960s, the most successful of which was B. Dalton, a bookstore chain that dominated the book market in suburban areas. Then in 1969, the Dayton Corporation merged with the J. L. Hudson Corporation based in Detroit, Michigan. Hudson was a prominent retailer in its own right, and the merging of the two companies created the Dayton Hudson Corporation, a retail giant that dominated in Minnesota and Michigan.

Nine years later, Dayton Hudson bought the retail chain Mervyn's and, in doing so, became the seventh largest retailer in the United States.

In 1983, the Daytons retired from their positions as heads of the company. But Dayton Hudson barreled along. The year 1990 brought yet another acquisition when Dayton Hudson bought powerhouse Chicago retailer Marshall Field's.

Dayton's Today

Over the years, Dayton's has established itself as the premier retailer in the United States. Mervyn's, Marshall Field's, and B. Dalton have been sold, but Target is going strong. In 2000, the Dayton Hudson Corporation became the Target Corporation, a name change that reflected the dominance of the Target brand. Today, more than 1,300 Target stores operate in 47 states. They bring in more than $40 billion annually and continue to promote George Dayton's community and philanthropic values. Through its education, arts, and other community programs, Target donates $2 million every week to various charitable causes.

The old Dayton's building still stands on Nicollet Avenue. Once Dayton's, then Marshall Field's, and now Macy's, it remains a nostalgic landmark for Minnesotans from all walks of life. In the words of former Minnesota governor Arne Carlson, "As long as I live, if there's a store there, I'll call it Dayton's."

Land of How Many Lakes?

We've managed to fit 37 of Minnesota's lovely lakes into this shape, which is roughly, approximately, sorta shaped like the wonderfully named Lake Winnibigoshish . . . but you can call it Lake Winnie; everyone else does. When you've found all 37, write down the unused letters from left to right, top to bottom, to find a hidden message with another fact about this watery wonderland.

Belle	Itasca	Reno
Bemidji	Kabetogama	Rush
Bush	Koronis	Sauk
Calhoun	Lake of the Isles	Saunders
Cass	Leech	Silver
Como	Long	Swan
Crystal	Loon	Toad
East Side	Mille Lacs	Traverse
Elbow	Minnetonka	Vermilion
Fish	Nokomis	Winnibigoshish
Gull	Otter Trail	Wolf
Harriet	Pelican	
Hiawatha	Rainy	

```
M
I H S I F
  N I N                                       E F
    G A S       D A O T                     O T L
      U W C S I N O R O K S A     A C H O
        L A K E O F T H E I S L E S T W
        U L T A O T T E R T R A I L
          H L H A R R I E T L H C
          O S S A U N D E R S Y O
  H O     U S U K A B E T O G A M A
  A S N R N C B N M E D G N O K O M I S
    H A E R A N O I L I M R E V L I S O
      C A R L O T B B S R L A T S Y R C
      I E E E O E I O T T C R   H A N
    N L J E L L N A W S S A     T E
  Y N E S D L N N G T A V H
    O P A E I U I S T E A
      N U W M M M I R D
        K L A K E S E
          S ! E B
```

For answers, turn to page 308.

Minnesotisms: The Basics

Minnesotans are people of few words, and that makes learning Minnesotan especially easy. With some simple instruction and a few basic terms you can speak like a native in no time.

Tip: Keep conversations short and, when possible, answer indirectly.

Term: Ya
Meaning: Yes
Example: Would you like some coffee?
Ya.

Term: If it's not too much trouble
Meaning: Yes (indirect form)
Example: Would you like another cup of coffee?
If it's not too much trouble.

Term: Then
Meaning: Sentence extender used to fill the space just before the period
Example: I've got a full pot in the kitchen.
I'll have another cup then.

Term: It's different
Meaning: Dislike (indirect form)
Example: Do you like the coffee? It's flavored with garlic. It's different.

Term: That's different
Meaning: Disapproval (indirect form)
Example: We bought the coffee from a guy pushing garlic at the State Fair.
That's different.

Term: Heckuva deal
Meaning: A good opportunity or bargain
Example: We got a heckuva deal on it. Five pounds for four dollars.

Term: You bet
Meaning: Used for emphasis of a point
Example: You bet, that's a heckuva deal.

Term: A guy
Meaning: A generic male (indirect form)
Example: I can see why a guy would buy five pounds at those prices.

Term: The wife
Meaning: What a husband calls his spouse
Example: Ya, the wife bought a couple of bags for Christmas presents.

Term: Not too bad
Meaning: Good (indirect form)
Example: Say, how is the wife?
Oh, not too bad.

Term: Could be worse
Meaning: Bad (indirect form)
Example: How's it going with your mother-in-law living with you then?
Oh, could be worse.

Term: Uff Da
Meaning: An exclamation used most often for emphasis at the beginning of a sentence
Example: Uff Da! It's cold outside!

Turn to page 264 for more Minnesotisms.

DID YOU KNOW?

Although the Dayton name is gone from department stores, it is still a part of life in Minnesota. In 2000, George Dayton's great-grandson Mark was elected to the U.S. Senate as a Democrat from Minnesota.

Of Ice and Men

Lace up your skates and join us to learn how professional ice hockey
has taken Minnesota for a roller-coaster ride for the last 40 years.

In 1966, the National Hockey League (NHL) decided to double its number of teams from six to twelve. The league's board of governors invited bids from interested states, and Minnesota was one of the first to apply. The bid was successful, and on February 9, 1966, the NHL granted Minnesota an expansion team slated to begin play in 1967.

Born in Bloomington

The new team needed a home, and location was key. The team's owners wanted a facility that was easily accessible from both Minneapolis and Saint Paul; they settled on Bloomington. Construction on the Metropolitan Sports Center, or the "Met," began soon after. Designed to accommodate approximately 15,000 spectators, the arena became one of the premier facilities of its time.

Six thousand season tickets sold immediately, and fans entered a contest to name their new team. People suggested the Norsemen, Muskies, Lumberjacks, and others, but in the end, the winning name was the Minnesota North Stars (in honor of the state motto).

The team lost its first game on the road, but in the home opener on October 21, 1967, the North Stars tied the Oakland Seals, another expansion team, in front of more than 13,000 fans. Spectators crowded inside the Met even though work crews were still installing seats.

Highs and Lows

The North Stars played well their first year and finished fourth in their division. This sent them to the playoffs where they beat the Los Angeles Kings but then lost to the Saint Louis Blues in a double-overtime semifinal.

This good first-year showing was marred by tragedy, however. In a game on January 13, 1968, forward Bill Masterton collided with an opposing defender and hit his head on the ice. Masterton lapsed into a coma and died two days later. His death remains the NHL's only on-ice fatality due to injury. To honor him, the league established the Bill Masterton Memorial Trophy, awarded annually to the NHL player who best exemplifies the qualities of perseverance, sportsmanship, and dedication to hockey.

From North Star to Lone Star

The Minnesota North Stars played in Bloomington for 27 years. They made the playoffs 17 times and won two conference championships. The team also played for the Stanley Cup twice: first in 1981, a loss to the New York Islanders; and again in 1991, a loss to the Pittsburgh Penguins.

Fans stayed loyal, but game attendance was down. In 1993, citing financial hardship, owner Norman Green moved the team to Texas, where the Minnesota North Stars became the Dallas Stars. Minnesotans were outraged and vilified Green, but the North Stars were gone.

Long Live the Wild

The state wouldn't be denied a professional hockey team for long, however. On June 25, 1997, four years after the North Stars left town, the NHL announced that it had awarded Minnesota another expansion franchise. Thanks to the Minnesota Wild, hockey was back in town.

Again, a new arena needed to be built, and the state legislated $65 million to help pay for the new facility. It's called the Xcel Energy Center and is located in Saint Paul.

Twelve thousand season tickets sold before a Wild game had even been played. And then finally, on September 29, 2000, Minnesotans cheered as the Wild took to the ice and played their first home game, beating the Anaheim Mighty Ducks 3–1.

Six years later, the team is thriving. In March 2003, the Wild made the playoffs, and in 2004, they hosted four World Cup games. Star players like Marian Gaborik, Pierre-Marc Bouchard, and Mikko Koivu thrill fans with their smart, energetic play, and coach Jacques Lemaire strives to take his team to the top. The North Stars may have deserted Minnesota for Texas, but the Wild seem here to stay.

Watkins by the Numbers

Before Amway, Tupperware, or Mary Kay, there was Watkins, a
Minnesota-based company that sold directly to consumers.

By the early 20th century, Watkins salesmen were familiar sights all over the Midwest, and some of their products (particularly vanilla extract and a topical pain reliever) remain popular today. Before it was a household name, however, Watkins was simply the surname of its founder, Joseph Ray "J. R." Watkins, who started the company in the late 1800s.

1/3

Amount of a Watkins product that customers can use and still get a money-back guarantee. In 1869, J. R. Watkins introduced the money-back guarantee and the Trial Mark bottle. Each Watkins bottle was marked with a line about one-third of the way from the top. J. R. encouraged customers to use the product to that mark and return it for a full refund if they weren't satisfied. Watkins was the first company to offer this service and continues to use the Trial Mark system today.

1

Product sold by the original Watkins Company; it was a topical pain reliever and anti-itch remedy called Watkins' Red

Liniment. The liniment's primary ingredients are camphor and capsicum (a red pepper plant), and it is still sold today.

6

Emmys won by the TV movie *Door to Door*, which told the story of Bill Porter, an Oregon-based Watkins salesman born with cerebral palsy. Porter began selling Watkins products in the 1960s and continues to sell them online and by phone.

28

Age at which J. R. Watkins moved to Plainview, Minnesota, and started cooking up home remedies in his kitchen.

110

Age of the Watkins Company when Minneapolis entrepreneur Irwin Jacobs bought it in 1978. J. R. died in 1911, and his heirs ran the company until Jacobs and his family took over.

350

Number of products Watkins offers today

$500

Cost of the first horse and buggy that J. R. Watkins used to deliver his products to customers. This door-to-door delivery service earned him the nickname "the Watkins Man." Subsequent Watkins salespeople were also called Watkins Men (and Women).

1895

Year Watkins started selling vanilla extract, black pepper, and cinnamon. The company's vanilla extract is especially popular with bakers because it is made from Madagascar Bourbon vanilla beans, considered by many people to be the most flavorful. Watkins vanilla is also more concentrated than other brands, so bakers need to use only half as much compared with other brands. To date, Watkins has sold about 13.5 million gallons of vanilla; that's enough to fill an Olympic-sized swimming pool 17 times.

1922

Year Watkins first offered "herbal supplements," or vitamins. The Watkins Company was the among the first in the United States to offer vitamin supplements for sale to the public.

45,000

Number of current Watkins employees

$1.2 million

Cost to build the Watkins administration building in 1912. The building features Tiffany-style glass, Italian tile and marble, and a 24-karat gold leaf rotunda ceiling. Located on Liberty Street in Winona, the building still houses Watkins's main offices and also features a small historical company museum.

The Mayo Clinic, Part II

The story of the Mayo brothers and their world-famous Rochester clinic continues. (Part I begins on page 32.)

Making It Big

In 1905, doctors at Saint Mary's Hospital performed 4,000 operations. By then, Dr. Will was the nation's leading authority on stomach surgery and that same year was named president of the American Medical Association.

Additions doubled the size of Saint Mary's twice, but the new beds filled up even before construction had finished. Rochester became a boomtown of sorts, burgeoning with hotels, restaurants, and boarding houses. The brothers thought about investing in the new businesses but instead chose to donate 10 percent of their profits to municipal improvements like paving roads and installing electricity in town.

Rules to Live By

The money the Mayos made came from the size of their practice, not from huge fees. They charged the same rates as any doctors in the Midwest. And they had a strict set of rules that they followed (and that their clinic still follows today):

- Never knowingly allow medical bills to become a burden to patients.

- Never sue to collect a fee.
- Never accept a promissory note, mortgage, or money raised by borrowing.
- Never let money affect the kind of care patients receive.

The Mayos' generosity also extended beyond their own hospital. Another medical first, the idea of granting advanced degrees in medical specialties, was the brainchild of officials at the University of Minnesota, but the school and its budget were too small to accommodate the program. So the Mayo brothers donated $1.5 million to the university for the project.

A Group Effort

In 1912, Mayo doctors saw 15,000 patients. By 1914, there were 17 senior physicians and 11 assistants on the diagnostic staff and almost as many on the surgical staff. By trusting in common sense and their belief in teamwork, the Mayos had pioneered a new kind of medical practice: the world's first group medical practice.

By this time, the Mayos' offices in downtown Rochester were spread throughout a three-block area interspersed with stores and restaurants. This made for so much confusion that the clinic had to hire full-time guides to lead patients from one office to another. What the practice needed was a new building.

The "Mayo Clinic" opened its doors on March 6, 1914.

Please, Not While I'm Eating

Even that facility soon proved too small. Rochester was growing to accommodate the increasing number of patients, some 60,000 a year by 1919. And so many of the city's visitors were clinic patients that signs hanging in restaurants all over town declared, "Please refrain from talking about your operation while eating!"

The Mayo Clinic grew apace. The hospital doubled in size; now it could hold 600 patients at one time. The clinic staff was nearing 500, and it was time to build a bigger clinic to house them all. The new 15-story building was finished in 1927 and went into operation in 1928.

Passing the Scalpel

Will retired from surgery that year, Charlie a year and a half later. The brothers withdrew from the practice gradually. In 1919, they set up the Mayo Foundation to run the clinic as a cooperative. This decision changed the clinic from a partnership to a self-governing association supported by a large endowment worth $10.5 million.

Immortality

Charlie died of pneumonia in 1939, and Will two months later of stomach cancer, the disease that had been his specialty. The two had built their lives and careers on service to others. Today, there are three Mayo Clinics: one in Jacksonville, Florida; one in Scottsdale, Arizona; and the original. All three operate according to the Mayos' principle: "The patient always comes first."

Bob Dylan

*This Minnesotan grew up to be one of America's
best-known singer-songwriters.*

Robert Allen Zimmerman was born on May 24, 1941, in
Duluth; he and his family moved to Hibbing six years later.
Although he tried to downplay his Midwestern roots for much
of his career, the region's influence on the man who became
Bob Dylan is unmistakable. Here are some things you may not
know about Dylan and his Minnesota connections.

Minnesota School Days

- Although the adult Bob Dylan is best known as a folk and
  protest singer, young Bobby Zimmerman stuck to more
  mainstream tunes. His first gig was singing "Accentuate the
  Positive" and "Some Sunday Morning" at a Mother's Day celebration in Duluth when he was five.
- Ten years later, he was so loud and raucous while performing "Rock 'n' Roll Is Here to Stay" at the 1957 school talent
  show that the Hibbing High principal pulled the plug on
  Dylan's microphone.

Minnesota Inspired

- Bob Dylan may be the University of Minnesota's most

famous dropout. He enrolled in 1959 but ignored the classroom in favor of playing folk music and hanging out at clubs in Dinkytown, Minneapolis's Bohemian neighborhood. Fourth Street bisects Dinkytown, and some Dylan watchers think it is this locale, and not the street of the same name in Greenwich Village, that Dylan memorializes in his 1965 song "Positively Fourth Street."

- Many people believe that Dylan's song "Girl of the North Country" was written for his high school girlfriend Echo Helstrom. Others, though, think the subject is activist Bonnie Beecher, whom Dylan knew in Minneapolis.

- "North Country Blues," from the 1963 album *The Times They Are A-Changin',* tells the story of mine closures and the families left unemployed as a result. This song is the most direct musical link between Dylan and his hometown; Hibbing endured its own mine closures and economic depression during the 1950s. One critic even called the song "an understated folk-epic of the history of Hibbing."

- The song "Highway 61 Revisited," from the 1965 album of the same name, takes its title from the road that leads from Duluth to Louisiana. This is the road young Robert Zimmerman took from Hibbing to college in Minneapolis.

- In 1974, Dylan returned to Minneapolis to rerecord with local musicians six songs cut from his album *Blood on the Tracks,* including one of his best-known tunes, "Tangled Up in Blue." He had composed most of the songs the previous summer while vacationing at his Minnesota farm.

Minnesota Memorials

- In 2002, Hibbing, Minnesota, launched Dylan Days, an annual festival staged during the week in May that coincides with the star's birthday. A literary night, a singer-songwriter competition, and an art show are among the Dylan Days activities.
- The house where Bob Dylan grew up is still a private residence and is not open to the public. But visitors on the Dylan Days' bus tour can roll by the place, which now stands on Bob Dylan Drive, the name the townspeople gave 7th Street in 2005.

DID YOU KNOW?

The Minnesota Wild's logo, a silhouetted profile of a bear's head, is rich with symbolism. Inside the silhouette, the sun setting over a forest depicts the Minnesota wilderness; the river that winds around to form the bear's mouth represents the state's many waterways; and the star as the animal's eye is in tribute to Minnesota's motto and the state's first professional hockey team.

Sculpture in the City

Part of the Walker Art Center, the first public art gallery in the upper Midwest, the Minnesota Sculpture Garden is a 15-acre site near downtown Minneapolis and is one of the largest urban sculpture gardens in the country.

Minneapolis has a reputation for attracting art lovers. The city is home to dozens of museums that feature oil paintings, watercolors, and other types of visual art. For sculpture, however, no place is better than the Minnesota Sculpture Garden, where more than 40 pieces are on permanent display and temporary exhibits keep the garden fresh. Here are some of the most popular.

Spoonbridge and Cherry, Claes Oldenburg and Coosje van Bruggen

The husband-and-wife sculpting team of Oldenburg and van Bruggen is responsible for the garden's signature work. This colossal bit of pop-art whimsy is a 29-foot-high, 7,000-pound fountain sculpture of a silver-white spoon and deep red cherry. The cherry gleams because of a thin spray of water from its stem, and the pair looks primed to meet an enormous ice cream sundae.

Arikidea, Mark di Suvero

"Wouldn't a rusty brown spider standing on a bed of fresh snow be great to behold?" sculptor Mark di Suvero asked himself. That question led to the creation of *Arikidea*, a piece that is more than 26 feet high and weighs about 3 tons. Made from I-beams discarded from New York City skyscrapers, the sculpture depicts an abstract arachnid. Of course, there isn't always snow on the ground, and not everyone sees the piece as a spider. One boy, asked to give the sculpture a name, called it "Twisted Steel Tripod." But there is one unusual feature about *Arikidea*: a wooden platform at its center sways with the slightest touch or breeze. Although many other sculptures in the garden are clearly marked with signs that say "Don't Touch," the decision to interact physically with this piece is left up to visitors.

Standing Glass Fish, Frank Gehry

This 1986 work by California artist and architect Frank Gehry captures motion as few sculptures do. Located inside the Cowles Conservatory (a three-sectioned greenhouse), the piece is a 22-foot-tall glass-and-silicone fish caught in an arching leap out of a lily pond. The work has personal meaning for Gehry. As a boy in Toronto, he often went with his grandmother to buy a large live carp at a local fish market. When they got home, young Frank watched the animal swim in the bathtub. Then, horrors! Grandma killed and cleaned the poor critter to make gefilte fish for her Friday night dinner. Gehry didn't like that ending, so this carp and the many other fish sculptures Gehry has created remain lively.

Hare on a Bell on Portland's Stone Piers, Barry Flanagan

This piece looks like part *Alice in Wonderland,* part Liberty Bell. Flanagan sculpted an elongated hare caught midair as it leaps over a cast-iron bronze bell. To some, the piece looks cartoonish, and the hare contrasts with the more formal look and shape of the bell. But Flanagan's sculpture is whimsical and fun, especially for young visitors.

Standing Frame, David Nash

This, as its title implies, is a big rectangular frame on a giant tripod. Although it looks like a dark bronze metal sculpture, the piece is actually made from two white oaks that Nash found near Taylors Falls, Minnesota. He later charred the wood to give it a metallic look. But what's the point of the big empty frame? The idea is that visitors can position themselves at different spots in the garden and look through the sculpture to frame the cityscape or whatever other view captures their fancy.

Two-Way Mirror Punched Steel Hedge Labyrinth, Dan Graham

Conceptual artist Graham's stainless steel piece not only has a mouthful of a title, it's also a house of mirrors. The piece is a geometric maze made up of walls with transparent and mirrored surfaces. Visitors can look at the work alone, but their reflections also become a part of the piece for others.

The Law and the Ludicrous

Be careful what you do and how you do it in Minnesota. This state has some laws that are bound to get people into trouble.

By the City

Here are some of the laws individual towns and cities have implemented:

- Men must grow beards in Brainerd.
- Women in Clearbrook nightclubs who weigh more than 200 pounds must stand more than five feet away from the bar to drink their drinks.
- Also in Clearbrook, it's illegal to play checkers at the airport.
- People who double-park in Minneapolis may be sent to a chain gang.
- It's illegal to drive a red car down Lake Street in Minneapolis.
- In Minnetonka, having a truck with dirty tires is a public nuisance.
- Cats in International Falls may not chase dogs up telephone poles.
- In Saint Cloud, men riding motorcycles must wear T-shirts.
- Also in Saint Cloud, you may not eat hamburgers on Sunday.

- Duluth does not allow people to let their dogs sleep in a barbershop, beauty salon, or bakery.

Throughout the State

Perhaps the cities take their example from the state? They aren't the only ones with laws a little on the odd side. In Minnesota, it's illegal to

- Cross the state line with a duck on your head.
- Tease skunks.
- Hang male and female underwear side by side on a clothesline.
- Sleep in the nude.
- Have sex with a live fish if you're a man.
- Use a telephone without parental supervision if you're under 12.

DID YOU KNOW?

Grace photographer Eric Enstrom took the first publicity pictures of a young Frances Gumm (Judy Garland) in the mid-1920s.

Charge!

Few moments during the Battle of Gettysburg were more heroic than the dramatic charge of the First Minnesota.

In April 1861, Minnesota's governor, Alexander Ramsey, was in Washington D.C., meeting with President Lincoln. When the Civil War began on April 12, Ramsey pledged his support to the new president and became the first governor to volunteer troops for the Union army. In July, one of those troop regiments, the First Minnesota Volunteer Infantry, saw combat at the Battle of Bull Run and was engaged in every major battle of the war thereafter. By the time the Union and Confederate armies converged outside the tiny town of Gettysburg, Pennsylvania, in July 1863, the men of the First Minnesota were veteran soldiers.

Setting the Stage

The Battle of Gettysburg was important for both sides. For the Union army, protecting the path to Washington, D.C., and other major northern cities was imperative. If the Confederates were able to capture the capital city or move into places like Philadelphia and New York, they would probably win the war. The Union troops surrounding Washington, D.C., and gathered in Gettysburg were all that stood between the enemy and victory.

For the Confederates, success at Gettysburg would be a certain morale booster. Robert E. Lee and his rebel troops were coming off of a dramatic win in Chancellorsville, Virginia. In May, a small contingent of Confederate troops had soundly defeated a large Union force there, and if Lee could also manage a win at Gettysburg, he might be able to take the North.

Troops from both sides met at Gettysburg on July 1, 1863, and the first day of fighting went badly for the Union. They were outnumbered and forced to retreat to the tops of two hills: Cemetery Ridge and Culp's Hill. Union commanders quickly realized, though, that controlling the high ground would give them a strategic position their enemy didn't have. So they spent the second day of the battle trying to secure their position on the hills. The fighting was fierce, and by the evening, things were looking grim for the Union army. One of the northern commanders had moved his troops off of the ridge in search of what he thought would be a better position. This left a gap through which the Confederate army could penetrate Union forces.

As 1,600 Confederates began marching unopposed toward the crest of Cemetery Ridge, the Union army started scrambling to move in reinforcements. They couldn't move fast enough, however, and there was little possibility of getting the troops to the hill before the rebels arrived. Union leaders feared that if they lost their position on Cemetery Ridge, their army's line would be broken, and they'd lose Gettysburg.

To Gain Five Minutes

At the crest, Union General Winfield Scott Hancock recognized immediately that he needed to stall the rebels. If he could gain just five extra minutes, he could move enough soldiers into place to protect the ridge. So Hancock turned to commander William Colville, leader of the First Minnesota. Hancock ordered Colville and his regiment to attack the charging rebels, who were, by then, only 100 yards away.

Hancock later said, "I had no alternative but to order the regiment in. I saw that in some way five minutes must be gained or we were lost. It was fortunate that I found such a grand body of men as the First Minnesota. I knew that they must lose heavily and it caused me pain to give the order for them to advance, but I would have done it if I had known every man would be killed. It was a sacrifice that must be made."

Courage Under Fire

Colville issued the order to the First Minnesota, and without hesitation, the 262 men charged, their bayonets drawn, down the hill and into the center of the Confederate forces. No one stopped for cover or even to fire a defensive shot.

The Confederates responded with a barrage of gunfire. Minnesota soldiers fell dead or injured with every step, but the unit focused only on moving forward. They knew they had to break through the line of fire and slow the Confederates to buy time for the Union army. As the First Minnesota reached the enemy's front line, the Southerners fell back, and the Minnesotans were able to take partial cover on the bank of a dry brook.

"The ferocity of our onset seemed to paralyze them for a time, and though they poured in a terrible and continuous fire from the front and enveloping flanks, they kept a respectful distance from our bayonets," wrote Lieutenant William Lochren of the First Minnesota Infantry.

Fighting continued, and the First Minnesota's flag fell five times. It always rose again, though, and ultimately, the infantry's mission was accomplished. The First Minnesota disrupted the enemy for some 15 minutes, long enough for reinforcement troops to arrive on Cemetery Ridge. That evening, the battle ended in a draw. The Union's luck changed the next day, and on July 4, Lee and his beleaguered Confederate army retreated south.

A Gallant Deed

The First Minnesota took heavy casualties at Gettysburg. Of the 262 men who attacked, all but 47 were killed or injured (a loss of some 82 percent). It was an important sacrifice, however, and General Hancock later praised the regiment, describing the charge as "one of the most gallant deeds in history."

DID YOU KNOW?

America's first Better Business Bureau was founded in Minneapolis in 1912.

Wait! Where Am I?

Minnesota has many towns whose names are more famous for being somewhere else. Take our quiz to see if you can identify them.

1. One of these towns better known for being in New Jersey is also a part of addresses in Minnesota. Do you know which one it is?
    A. Newark
    B. Hackensack
    C. Cherry Hill
    D. Cape May

2. Texas? New York? We should say not! Which two towns can be found in Minnesota?
    A. Southfork and Yonkers
    B. El Paso and Staten Island
    C. Austin and Buffalo
    D. San Antonio and Syracuse

3. And you thought Minnesota only ripped off town names. Which states actually appear as towns in the North Star State?
    A. Virginia
    B. Nevada
    C. Maine
    D. All of the above

4. Ah, Leavenworth. Fertile fields. Rolling prairies. Federal prison? Lest we not get confused, identify the fact or facts about the town of Leavenworth, Minnesota.

    A. The population hovers just above 300.

    B. Johnny Cash played a concert there.

    C. It was established by an act of Congress in 1895.

    D. All of the above

5. Minnesota isn't known as the "home of presidents," but which presidential palace is also the name of a Minnesota town?

    A. Monticello

    B. Mount Vernon

    C. Ash Lawn

    D. Peacefield

For answers, turn to page 308.

DID YOU KNOW?

The Minnesota State Fair is the third most-attended fair in the United States.

The Little City
That Could

From its humble beginnings as a fur trading post, through
abandonment, resurgence, abandonment, and resurgence, the
northeastern city of Duluth has grown into a major city
on Lake Superior, Minnesota's "unsalted sea."

Town: Duluth
Location: Saint Louis County
Founding: 1856
Current population: 86,919
Size: 87.3 square miles
Median age: 35.4 years
County seat: Yes

What's in a Name?
Duluth is named for the Frenchman who claimed the area for
France in 1679: Daniel Greysolon Du Lhut.

Claims to Fame:
- Duluth was settled, abandoned, and resettled many times
  during its history. Native Americans and the French
  explored the area as early as the 17th century. In 1809,
  German immigrant John Jacob Astor built a fur trading

company on the site of present-day Duluth. That fort was abandoned in the 1840s, and the area remained quiet until rumors of a lucrative mine reached Eastern settlers. In 1853, Duluth was resettled after a treaty with the Ojibwa Indians opened the area. It would be 15 years, though, before Duluth really came into its own. The year 1868 brought the railroad, and on July 4, newspaperman Thomas Foster declared Duluth the "Zenith City of the Unsalted Seas." By 1870, the city's population had swelled to 3,500.

- Police in Duluth issued the city's first speeding ticket in 1872. Mr. Trowbridge, the gentleman who received the ticket, was driving his wagon team faster than the allowed speed limit of "the walking gait of a man." Trowbridge's fine was five dollars.

- In 1890, the Merritt brothers from Duluth, also called the "Seven Iron Men," were the first people to open an iron mine in the Mesabi Range.

- Duluth and neighboring Superior, Wisconsin (dubbed the Twin Ports), share one of the largest freshwater ports in the world.

DID YOU KNOW?

In 1972, Minnesota doctor Paul Ellwood coined the term "health maintenance organization," or HMO.

Swedes Built This City

Approximately 60 percent of the Swedish immigrants to 19th century America settled in the Midwest, many of those in Minnesota. In fact, by 1900, Minnesota was home to more than 60,000 Swedes, the largest Swedish population in the United States. Of those, 26,000 made the Twin Cities their home. In Saint Paul, the majority of Swedish immigrants settled in east Saint Paul, in a section of town called Swede Hollow.

Welcome to the Hollow

Early Swedish settlers named the area *Svenska Dallen,* or "Swedish Dale." That name evolved over the years into "Swede Hollow." But the people who lived there called it simply "the Hollow."

Immigrants arrived in the Hollow by train. They rode steam engines from eastern port cities to Saint Paul's original Union Depot and then walked up the tracks in search of relatives in the neighborhood. Many new arrivals spoke no English and wore notes pinned to their coats to identify them.

Life in the Hollow was tough. Residents' homes had few, if any, amenities. A creek wound through town and acted both as a water source and a sewage system. Many Hollowites built outhouses right on the river. One resident wrote, "[The privy] was built over the creek on stilts . . . Every time you'd get a heavy rain, that would make this very sedate creek a rushing torrent, and many of the privies would end up at the far end of the Hollow . . . and would have to be retrieved by their owners."

Not Just for Swedes Anymore

By the early 20th century, many of the original Swedish settlers had moved out; they saved money and managed to move to nicer neighborhoods. But the Hollow itself remained a "stepping-stone" neighborhood for many immigrants. From the 1850s to the 1950s, Swede Hollow was home to several immigrant groups, including the Irish, Italians, Mexicans, and, of course, the original Swedes.

A Thriving Slum

By all accounts, Swede Hollow was a disorganized slum. The town wasn't arranged according to any logical scheme. There was no grid pattern to its alleys or roads. The houses were built closely together. No one had electricity. And most families lived in tar-paper shacks crowded with dozens of relatives.

Yet the neighborhood thrived. Residents engaged in the cultural traditions of their homelands and took pride in their new community. The Swedes cooked elaborate Scandinavian meals. The Italians made their own wine; one man who grew up in the Hollow remembered his father and other men singing as they crushed grapes with their feet. Families tended gardens and raised animals on any open space they could find. And they were creative with food; during the Great Depression, some families ate dandelions at every meal.

Most of the Hollow's residents didn't even realize they lived in a slum. One man wrote that he didn't know his hometown was a "slum" until he saw a historical society video that labeled it as such. While he lived there, he said, "That was the best place to be!"

Razing the Hollow

The city of Saint Paul disagreed. During the 1950s, the Twin Cities undertook massive urban renewal projects in an effort to keep families from moving to suburbs. One of the sections of town that caught the eye of city officials was Swede Hollow. Residents of the Hollow did not pay property taxes; thus, the city did not provide any services. As such, the primitive living conditions health inspectors discovered when they visited the area were deemed unacceptable. The lack of sewer and water facilities was horrifying, they said, and many of the Hollow's children suffered from whooping cough and pneumonia.

In 1956, the city evicted Swede Hollow's last 16 families. They were relocated, but the places to which they were sent were little better than their Hollow homes. One family couldn't even stay together as city officials found them a flat with room for only five of their ten children. Then, on December 11, 1956, with all residents removed, the Saint Paul Fire Department covered the Hollow's shacks with gasoline and burned them to the ground.

Today, the area is a park that visitors can access from Payne Avenue. The houses are gone, but remnants of their foundations and gardens remain along the walking and biking paths that wind through what once was Swede Hollow.

Stassen the Stalwart

*Lots of people make fun of Minnesota politician Harold Stassen.
Yes, he ran for the presidency nine times between 1948 and 1992 and
never won. And yes, he sometimes wore a hairpiece to make himself look
younger and, therefore, more appealing to voters. But the jokes stop
there. Here are five things you likely didn't know about the
man often mislabeled "Minnesota's biggest loser."*

1. He was one smart cookie.

Stassen was born in South Saint Paul in April 1907. He graduated from Humboldt High School in 1921 and then from law
school at the University of Minnesota in 1929. Are you doing
the math? He was 14 when he ended his high school career
and 22 when he earned a law degree and went into private
practice.

2. He was Minnesota's youngest governor.

In 1938, at the age of 31, Stassen was elected governor of
Minnesota. He remains the youngest person to hold that title,
an office he won twice more in 1940 and 1942.

3. He was a war hero.

While his political comrades stayed home to solidify their
constituencies during World War II, Stassen resigned as
Minnesota's governor and joined the U.S. Navy in 1943. He

served in the Pacific, where he was decorated three times, won six major battle stars, and acted as the head of the navy's prisoner evacuation program in Japan. President Franklin D. Roosevelt also chose Stassen to be a delegate to the 1945 United Nations Charter Conference in San Francisco.

4. He liked Ike.

Stassen wore several hats in the Eisenhower White House. He was a cabinet and National Security Council member, and he was the chief American negotiator during the 1957 London arms control negotiations.

5. He marched with King.

In 1963, Harold Stassen joined Civil Rights leader Martin Luther King Jr. in the March on Washington. Stassen, a lifelong Republican, developed a reputation as a liberal during the 1960s for his strong belief in civil rights.

DID YOU KNOW?

In December 1889, the Minneapolis Public Library was the first library to separate children's books from the rest of the collection.

Superior's Shipwrecks

Minnesota has profited greatly from shipping along the waterways of Lake Superior. Yet what the lake giveth, it also taketh away. Here are some of the state's most memorable maritime disasters.

The *Samuel P. Ely*: October 29–30, 1896

Towed by the stout steamer the *Hesper*, the *Ely* left Duluth on the morning of October 29, 1896, on a routine trip to pick up a load of iron ore from Two Harbors, some 25 miles away. The trip should have taken only a few hours, but a storm over the lake churned up high seas and whirling winds, and the *Ely* and *Hesper* took more than eight hours to make the trip. By the time they arrived at Two Harbors, the storm was a violent force that threatened to sink both boats. To save itself, the *Hesper* cast off the tow line, setting the *Ely* free and leaving it to toss helplessly in the savage swells. The *Ely* crashed into the breakwater, and the terrified crew clung to the ship's rigging throughout the night as rescuers on shore tried to devise the safest way to save the men. The next morning, locals gathered to watch as a small sailboat ventured onto the lake to pick up the sailors, a couple at a time.

All hands were saved, but the ship was a total loss. The owners hired a crew to strip the ship of its sailing equipment, and the picking apart of the *Ely* continued for decades. During the 1950s and 1960s, divers removed anchors and other items to decorate private lawns and fill local museums. Then, in the early 1960s, a diving service let tourists visit the *Ely* and take home a set of dishes from the wreck. A reporter soon discovered, however, that the company was running a scam, planting dishes bought from Goodwill on the boat. The diving service closed, but the *Ely* still rests roughly 35 feet below the surface off the coast of Two Harbors.

The *Niagara*: June 4, 1904

The *Niagara* was an innovation. It was built in 1872 as one of several large "outside" tug boats that traveled outside harbors and onto Lake Superior's open waters. The *Niagara* had weathered Great Lakes storms for more than 30 years when it finally met its fate at Knife Island.

A malfunctioning compass led the *Niagara* astray, and the boat slammed into the island's rocks. With waves pounding it into the rocks, the tug quickly began to come apart. Crew members sent out a distress call heard in a tiny town nearby. The telegraph operator there relayed a message to Two Harbors, where rescuers dispatched a tug called the *Edna G.* to come to the *Niagara's* aid. The *Edna G.* managed to rescue all 13 passengers, and amazingly, there was only one injury: a female passenger cut her hand on some broken glass while trying to escape.

The *Madeira* and the *Edenborn*: November 28, 1905

One of the worst storms in Minnesota history blew onto Lake Superior in November 1905. The storm dumped several inches of snow and battered the state with 60 mph winds. Ships caught on Lake Superior during the storm were in terrible danger, and the *Madeira*, towed by the steamer *William Edenborn*, was one of 20 that were damaged or destroyed.

At about three-thirty in the morning on November 28, amidst violent winds and churning water, the captain of the *Edenborn* decided to cut the *Madeira* free, believing both ships would have a better chance of survival on their own. The attempt was for naught, however. The *Edenborn* ran aground and broke in two near the town of Split Rock; four miles away, the *Madeira* crashed into a rocky cliff.

While the *Edenborn's* crew waited on shore for rescue, the *Madeira* was breaking apart fast, and her crew was in peril. But crewman Fred Benson grabbed some line, jumped off the ship and onto a rocky outcropping, climbed a 60-foot cliff, and threw the line back down to the sinking ship. One by one, the *Madeira's* crew climbed to safety, and all but one man survived.

Two days later, the *Edna G.* made two more successful rescues. The tug picked up the crews of both the *Madeira* and the *Edenborn*, but the ships were lost. In response to the accident, the Split Rock lighthouse was erected not far from the spot where the Madeira ran aground.

In 1955, a Duluth diving group called the "Frigid Frogs" discovered the exact location of the *Madeira's* wreckage. It remains a popular diving spot.

The *Onoko*: September 15, 1915
It was a clear, calm September day when the *Onoko* left Duluth harbor with a load of grain. The ship grounded on the way out

of the harbor but freed itself and continued on. A few days later, on September 15, an engineer noticed water filling the engine room. Within a few minutes, the ship had sunk. The crew all escaped into lifeboats, but the circumstances surrounding the sinking were suspicious. Some argued that the accidental grounding a few days earlier caused unseen damage; others claimed foul play. World War I was raging in Europe, and, according to some crewmen, an Austrian passenger had acted strangely, repeatedly commenting on the poor condition of the boat. In the end, investigators rejected the war plot theory, and the wreck of the *Onoko* was ruled an accident.

The *Edmund Fitzgerald*: November 10, 1975

The most well-known maritime disaster to occur on Lake Superior was that of the *Edmund Fitzgerald*. Carrying a load of iron ore, the ship left the Duluth-Superior Harbor without incident, but on the way to Michigan, a storm quickly gathered on the lake. Ten-foot waves soon pounded the deck, and winds blew at 35 knots. The radio operator on the *Fitzgerald* contacted a nearby ship, the *Arthur M. Anderson,* and reported flooding, downed railings, and radar problems.

Communication between the two ships continued, and the *Fitzgerald's* operator reported that they were "holding our own." That was the last communiqué anyone received from the *Edmund Fitzgerald*. The ship, her crew of 29, and her cargo vanished into the lake. The Coast Guard found the wreckage a few days later and it has been explored extensively, but exactly what caused the ship to founder remains a mystery.

Sometimes the Sailor's a Wreck

- In November 1926, Minnesota seaman Charles Smith had had enough. Shortly after his ship departed Duluth, a storm confined him to his cabin on the *Cuyler Adams* for the entire day. With an increasingly growling stomach, he suddenly announced to his fellow sailors that he "might as well die of too much water as too little food," and began to make his way to the mess hall. As he walked across the ice-coated deck, a large wave crested over the side and swept him out to sea.

- Too much food can also be bad. In 1937, while loading oats into the hold of the steamer *W .J. Connors,* Wesley Taylor fell into the hold. No one noticed, and the ship left Duluth harbor at full steam, heading for Buffalo, New York. Taylor managed to dig himself out and began banging on the wall of the hold; crewmen heard this, became alarmed, and returned the ship to port. After the crew removed 4,000 bushels of oats, they found Taylor uninjured. His time in the oats had whet Taylor's appetite; he immediately ate dinner aboard the ship and then went home to recuperate.

- The successful Minnesota Atlantic Transit Company named all of its ships after playing cards (*Ace, King, Queen, Jack, Ten,* and *Nine*) and had every reason to believe it had a winning hand. Yet the rank-and-file sailors knew better. The fleet was cursed, they believed, and the captains got the worst of it. One captain was mowed down by a car on the way back to his ship; another was torpedoed during World War II; and a third died in a car crash in Detroit.

Am I Blue?

This little town on the prairie has made a big name for itself.

Town: Blue Earth
Location: Faribault County
Founding: 1855
Current population: 4,000
Size: 3.2 square miles
Median age: 44 years
County seat: Yes

What's in a Name?

The Native Americans called the river nearby *Mahkota* (or "Blue Earth") because its high banks were replete with blue-black clay. When settlers arrived, they decided to name the new town after the river.

Claims to fame:

- You think all Eskimos come from Alaska? Think again. The Eskimo Pie got its start in Blue Earth. Back in 1917, a local man named Walter Schwen patented the Chocolate Dream, a vanilla ice cream bar dipped in chocolate candy. He later sold the patent to Chicago salesmen Christian K. Nelson and Russell Stover. Nelson renamed the Chocolate Dream, calling it an Eskimo Pie, and sold the treat all over the country. Russell Stover got out of the ice cream business and opened his own candy company.

- Blue Earth sits at the midpoint of I-90, America's longest interstate highway. I-90 stretches more than 3,000 miles from Boston, Massachusetts, to Seattle, Washington. A driver traveling at 65 mph from either Boston or Seattle would need about 46 hours to make the entire trip, and that's if he never stopped for snacks, gas, or a visit to the loo. Around hour 23, he'd arrive in Blue Earth.

- At the midpoint of I-90 is the world's tallest statue of the Jolly Green Giant. Made of fiberglass, the Giant stands about 55 feet tall and watches over some of Minnesota's most fertile farmland.

- Blue Earth's Good Shepherd Episcopal Church has changed very little since it was constructed in 1871. And the center window over the altar, the one showing Christ as the Good Shepherd, was the first stained-glass window brought to Minnesota.

DID YOU KNOW?

Minnesota-born musician Prince taught himself to play 20 musical instruments, including the piano, guitar, bass, drums, and keyboard.

Marquee Minnesota

Minnesota has an impressive list of accomplished favorite sons and daughters. You've seen their movies and TV shows, read their books, and heard their songs. To find four of their well-known titles, just fill in the blank squares!

ACROSS

1 *Wuthering Heights* setting
6 Dance in a '90s rock club
10 Jiffs
14 Sleep disorder
15 Two-tone cookie
16 Jacob's twin
17 Considers
18 Meter maid of song
19 Reply to "That a fact?"
20 1987 comedy from Minneapolis's Joel and Ethan Coen
23 Diarist Anaïs
24 Intensify
25 1960s legal drama starring Owatonna's E. G. Marshall
31 Mississippi, e.g.
32 Poet Marianne
33 Newman role
36 Wrapped up
37 Jetties
38 Submerged
39 The first word of Dante's *Inferno*

40 "King of Torts" Melvin
41 Got going
42 2005 medical drama with Minneapolis's T. R. Knight
44 Sharp, piercing cry
47 Altar-cloth linen
48 1925 novel by Saint Paul's F. Scott Fitzgerald
54 Atari game
55 Twofold
56 Like most owls
58 *The Clan of the Cave Bear* author
59 "Rule, Britannia" composer
60 Iranian bread
61 Genealogical chart
62 Movie shot
63 Got some Z's

DOWN

1 Satirical comic
2 Letters on a phone button
3 Most eligible, in a way
4 String on a finger, e.g.
5 More cheeky

6   Before noon, to poets
7   Not a dup.
8   ___ good example
9   Pack rats and magpies
10   Confiscates
11   Legally bar
12   Queeg's ship
13   Lazy girl?
21   File extension
22   "Able was ___..."
25   1982 Disney film and
     video game
26   Honey bunch?
27   First name in stunts
28   Poet Dickinson
29   Holiday airs
30   *Andrea* ___: famed ship
33   Science fiction award
34   Great Seal motto word
35   Familiar designer initials
37   Spied on
38   Weighs anchor
40   ___ Rabbit
41   Fishermen, at times
42   Tickled response
43   Cagers' org.
44   Ireland's patron, briefly
45   D-Day time
46   Actress Zellweger
49   Kind of glow around one
50   Aquarium
51   High spirits
52   Hillside, in Scotland
53   Pound sound
57   It lasts from Apr. to Oct.

For answers, turn to page 309

~ 205 ~

Sinclair Lewis

Author and Minnesotan Sinclair Lewis was the first American to win a Nobel Prize for literature in 1930. Four years earlier, he had been the first person to refuse a Pulitzer Prize.

Harry Sinclair Lewis was born on February 7, 1885, in Sauk Centre, Minnesota. His father, a country doctor, has been described as cold and impersonal. His mother died of tuberculosis when Harry was six years old. His father remarried a year later, and Harry was close to his stepmother. She read to him and instilled in him a love of literature.

Harry's youth and adolescence were trying times. Socially awkward, unpopular, and marked by bright red hair, he found solace in books and kept a diary as a boy. He eventually went to Yale University where he worked on the school's literary magazine and graduated in 1908. In 1912, Lewis published his first novel, *Hike and Aeroplane,* under a pseudonym, though he held a number of jobs before devoting himself to writing full time. When he did, he crafted tales about small-town life—in particular, small-town Minnesota life—that won him both acclaim from critics and scorn from his hometown.

Here is a list of Lewis's major accomplishments, by the books.

Main Street

In 1920, Lewis published *Main Street,* a scathing satire of small-town life, and caused an immediate sensation. Set in fictional Gopher Prairie, Minnesota, a thinly disguised Sauk Centre, the book attacked the Middle American way of life and exposed what Lewis believed was its bigotry, hypocrisy, and conformity.

Main Street is centered on the character of Carol Kennicott, a young woman who moves to Gopher Prairie after marrying a simple country doctor. Instead of the warm and friendly rustic life that match the idyllic image her husband has painted, she finds a town filled with judgmental, meddling, gossipy neighbors. Although she tries to embrace small-town life, Carol finds it stultifying and seeks out a larger city. That isn't much better. As prominent author and critic H. L. Mencken put it, *Main Street* is "an attempt, not to solve the American cultural problem, but simply to depict with great care a group of typical Americans. This attempt is extraordinarily successful."

Even so, Lewis's Minnesota neighbors were none too pleased with his portrayal of their lives. The book was banned in the town of Alexandria. In Sauk Centre, the library also banned it for a time, and it was more than six months before the *Sauk Centre Herald* even acknowledged its existence.

Babbitt

In 1922, Lewis' second major novel, *Babbitt,* was published, and it was an even greater success than *Main Street* had been. *Babbitt* tells the story of a businessman named George F. Babbitt who, though yearning for greater fulfillment than can be found in material goods, still falls prey to commercialism and conformity. The novel gave the world a new term: "Babbitt," which refers to "a business or professional man who conforms unthinkingly to prevailing middle-class standards."

Arrowsmith

Sinclair Lewis's third major novel, *Arrowsmith,* was published in 1925. It portrays the life of a doctor trying to maintain his integrity amid the quackery, commercialism, and bureaucratic politics of medical schools, hospitals, and the Department of Public Health. Unlike Sinclair's two previous novels, this book's hero retains his ethical standards.

It was for *Arrowsmith* that Sinclair Lewis was awarded the Pulitzer Prize, but he declined it. Many people believe that Lewis refused the prize out of resentment for his earlier novels not having been so honored. *Main Street* had been a contender for the Pulitzer in 1921, but the honor went instead to Edith Wharton for *The Age of Innocence.* Lewis, though, wrote that his refusal stemmed from his disapproval of contests that praised one book over another or called a single work, as the Pulitzer committee did, the "best novel of the year." Who could possibly be competent to select one novel as the "best," he wondered.

Elmer Gantry

The publication of *Elmer Gantry* in 1927 once again drew Sinclair Lewis into controversy. This time, people were so enraged that they threatened him with bodily harm. The book, a fierce castigation of hypocrisy in revivalist religion, was denounced by clergymen of all faiths and was banned in Boston.

The Nobel committee, however, was not so affected. Three years later, in 1930, Lewis was awarded the Nobel Prize for Literature "for his vigorous and graphic art of description and his ability to create, with wit and humour, new types of characters." Lewis was the first American to be so honored, and this prize he accepted graciously.

Lewis continued to publish novels (23 in all) until his death in 1951. And although he remained popular throughout his life, he never again achieved the critical success of his most productive years.

DID YOU KNOW?

Although several of his novels angered the residents of his hometown, Sinclair Lewis has, in the years since his death, been embraced by Sauk Centre. The town now boasts a Sinclair Lewis Interpretive Center and Boyhood Home and Sinclair Lewis Park (where band concerts are held). The town also sponsors annual Sinclair Lewis Days and the Sinclair Lewis Writers' Conference.

Haunted Happenings: The Milford Mine

It's a mining mystery that still haunts the residents of Crow Wing County. Just what happened inside the Milford mine?

The Spook:

Clinton Harris

What Happened?

In Crow Wing County, 200 feet underground in the Cuyana range, is the site of one of Minnesota's worst mining disasters. On February 5, 1924, miners working in a shaft of the Milford mine set off a dynamite blast. It blew through the wall of the shaft and into a nearby pond, sending a wall of water rushing into the mine. Miners raced for the surface, struggling through knee-deep and then waist-deep water in an effort to get out. Only seven emerged. Forty-one men were still trapped inside.

One of those was Clinton Harris, who was working deep in the shaft when the mine flooded. When the disaster struck, Harris sounded a bell to warn men above of the accident. For hours after the mine filled with water, that warning bell continued to ring. Finally, someone disconnected it.

Three months passed before any bodies could be recovered. Workers first had to drain the pond and then pump all of the water out of the mine. When they did, they discovered the remains of all 41 men, Clinton Harris included.

For Whom the Bell Tolls?

The story should have ended there. When the mine reopened and workers went back inside, 12 men traveled to the 200-foot depth, planning to go back to their jobs of excavating iron ore. But at the bottom of the shaft, the men caught a glimpse of a shadowy figure. They raised their lanterns to get a better look and saw the ghost of Clinton Harris, decayed and transparent, standing in the shaft, the warning bell's cord tied around his waist.

Those miners wasted no time returning to the surface. They scrambled up a wooden ladder and spilled outside as a phantom warning bell sounded below.

Mining continued at Milford for several years. But many miners, after hearing the story of Clinton Harris, refused to continue working there.

For more haunted happenings, turn to page 227.
To read about Minnesota mining, turn to page 56.

DID YOU KNOW?

Northern Minnesota is close enough to the North Pole that it's possible to see the aurora borealis. The dancing lights can last from a few minutes to several hours, and although summer is the best time to see them, keen eyes can catch them any time of the year.

What a Ham!

Some cultures give us delicacies—foie gras, escargot.
Minnesota gave us Spam.

Hormel, the meat-packing company in Austin, Minnesota, developed the first canned ham in 1926. It was called "Hormel Flavor-Sealed Ham." That was fine, as far as it went, but the cans still had to be refrigerated. What the world really needed, Hormel execs decided, was a meat product that could live on a shelf without ever needing to see the inside of an icebox.

Spice Spice, Baby

So Jay C. Hormel, the son of Hormel's founder, George A. Hormel, concocted a meaty mixture that didn't need to be refrigerated. The ingredients included pork shoulder, ham, and a bunch of spices ("secret" spices, the company maintains). Jay Hormel called the new dish "Hormel Spiced Ham."

The stuff actually tasted good, everyone agreed, but the name lacked a certain pizzazz. To make matters worse, other meat-packing companies, recognizing what a great idea the spiced ham was, began marketing their own versions, eating into Hormel's profits. Something had to be done.

So the folks at Hormel held a contest and offered $100 to

whomever could come up with a jazzy name for the new meat product. The winning entry, submitted by Kenneth Daigneau, an actor who just happened to be the brother of a Hormel executive, was "Spam" ("SPiced hAM"). In 1937, the first cans of Spam made their way from the Hormel factories to American tables.

Singing Its Praises

The folks at Hormel didn't just rely on the new name to speak to the population at large. They launched a major advertising campaign. In 1940, they came up with a musical commercial to promote the product. The jingle went

Spam Spam Spam Spam
Hormel's new miracle meat in a can
Tastes fine, saves time,
If you want something grand,
Ask for Spam.

A Bite of Spam, Mr. Khrushchev?

The advertising blitz worked. When Spam sponsored the hugely popular *George Burns and Gracie Allen Show* and was promoted by its stars, the product's popularity soared. Spam was cheap and satisfying, just the thing people needed in those difficult prewar days.

The start of World War II further boosted the new food-stuff's popularity. Since it needed no refrigeration, Spam was the perfect food for soldiers to take into battle, and they developed a taste for it. At home, it wasn't rationed the way beef was, so Spam became a staple on the American table.

Hormel also donated millions of cans of Spam to U.S. Allies during the war. In *Khrushchev Remembers,* the former Soviet premier goes so far as to credit Spam with the survival of the Russian Army during World War II.

The Monty Python Connection

Over the years, Spam gained much notoriety. *Monty Python's Flying Circus* even performed a skit that has entered the annals of Spam lore.

A group of Vikings sits in a cafe. Whenever the word Spam is uttered, they sing and chant " Spam, Spam, Spam," etc. growing louder as they go. A customer (played by Eric Idle) enters with his wife (Graham Chapman in drag). A waitress (Terry Jones, also in drag) approaches to take their order. Everything on the menu contains Spam, but the wife does not like Spam. With the chanting Vikings repeating the Spam song each time the product is mentioned, the zany sketch pointed out the ubiquitous nature of Spam.

The Monty Python connection did not end there. When Python regular Eric Idle decided to update the group's 1975 movie, *Monty Python and the Holy Grail,* and turn it into a musical, he chose as his title, *Monty Python's Spamalot.* Why? Because, said Idle, "Spam is the holy grail of canned meats." After a successful debut in Chicago, the show opened at the Shubert Theater in New York on March 17, 2005, and became one of Broadway's most popular shows.

Spam on the Net

With the growing use of the Internet, the word "spam" came to be associated with the practice of UCE (unsolicited commercial e-mail). This was a direct result of the Monty Python comedic sketch. Hormel's Web site explains:

> Use of the term "Spam" was adopted as a result of the Monty Python skit in which a group of Vikings sang a chorus of " Spam, Spam, Spam . . . " in an increasing crescendo, drowning out other conversation. Hence, the analogy applied because UCE was drowning out normal discourse on the Internet.

In 2002, Hormel sued a British company called Antilles Landscapes Investments over their trademark anti-spam product, Spambuster. Hormel lost the case, though Antilles did have to pay Hormel £1,000 (about $1,500) to defray its court expenses. Regarding Hormel's complaint, the English court's decision noted, in part,

> The proposition that someone who encounters computer programming services under the mark Spambuster would think any less of the applicants' luncheon meat product or be discouraged from purchasing that product is more than a little fanciful.

Spam I Am

Over the years, Hormel has introduced new versions of its meat product. In addition to original Spam, there is now Oven Roasted Turkey Spam, Spam Smoke Flavored, Spam Lite, and Spam Less Sodium. Hormel assures us that all still have the great Spam taste. As of July 2002, Hormel had shipped more than 6 billion cans of Spam worldwide.

All that spicy meat goes into the bellies of many dedicated Spam lovers. For them, Hormel also engages in many Spam fan services. The company runs an interactive Web site with Spam poetry, Spam puzzles, and Spam merchandise. There is also a Spam fan club and a Spammobile that crisscrosses the country to acquaint Americans with the great taste of Spam.

To read about Austin, Minnesota (the home of Spam), turn to page 248.

DID YOU KNOW?

Hawaiians consume more Spam than residents of any other state. There is even a Hawaiian specialty called Spam musubi, a kind of Spam sushi. Here is how one aficionado describes the dish:

Well, you take a slice of fried Spam, which has been marinated in a special sauce, place it on top of formed and sticky sushi rice and wrap a piece of seaweed, or nori, around it to hold it all together. It's like sushi. OK, it's pretty much like sushi. Except it's not fish. And the Spam is fried. So you can't call it raw. Which makes it not so much like sushi. But whatever . . .

The dish is so popular in Hawaii that there are even competitions for the longest Spam musubi. The record, so far, is an incredible 300 feet, the length of a football field. Now that's just Spam-tastic!

A Pioneering Childhood

Long before J. K. Rowling imagined Harry Potter, another author
captured the imagination of both children and adults with her books.
Laura Ingalls Wilder wrote the hugely popular Little House series
about her childhood travels across the American plains.

Laura Ingalls Wilder started her writing career in the twilight of her life. Her daughter, Rose, a journalist, encouraged Laura to write about traveling through the Midwest by covered wagon with her family. Although Laura had written articles for the *Missouri Ruralist* and the *Saint Louis Star*, it wasn't until 1930, when she was 63 years old, that she began her first book.

In 1932, *Little House in the Big Woods* was published. It was essentially an autobiographical tale of Laura's early years with her family in Wisconsin. Even though she took some artistic license, Laura wrote about real people and actual events. The book was tremendously popular, and Laura followed up with six more volumes describing her life as a pioneer girl and one about the life of her husband, Almanzo Wilder.

Westward Ho!

On the Banks of Plum Creek, the fourth book of the series, begins with the Ingalls family stopping its covered wagon on the flatlands of western Minnesota. Laura's parents, Charles and Caroline, bought 172 acres of fertile prairie land in North Hero

Township, Redwood County, Minnesota. Their property was two miles north of Walnut Grove, a town comprised of a few stores and houses scattered around the railroad tracks on the prairie.

The Ingalls family's first home in Minnesota was a tiny house dug into the bank of a stream called Plum Creek. Years later, Laura described the dugout as "a funny little house to move into." Because the prairie was treeless, settlers often constructed dugouts and shelters out of sod. Laura wrote, "It had only one room, dug into the creek bank like a cave. Willows had been laid over it and grass sods laid on them; the grass grew tall and thick on this roof, which looked exactly like the rest of the prairie."

At the end of the long Minnesota winter, Charles planted a wheat crop. Optimistic about the territory's rich, fertile land, he purchased wood on credit at the lumberyard. In the spring of 1875, Charles built a frame house replete with glass windows, factory-milled doors, and white china doorknobs. Laura called the home "the wonderful house" when the family moved into it from the dugout across the creek.

A Plague on Both Her Houses

Life in the wonderful house looked promising, but that didn't last long. One summer day in 1875, what at first looked to be a fast-moving thundercloud turned out to be a horde of locusts. The locusts fell to the ground like hail and devoured everything in their path. Within hours, the wheat in the fields, the vegetables in the garden, the plums along the creek, the leaves and grass of the prairie were gone. Laura wrote that the locust invasion was "the worst ever known since the plagues of

Egypt." The Ingalls family was left in debt and with little food. In order to support them, Charles walked more than 200 miles to eastern Minnesota to find work as a harvest hand. At the end of the summer, he returned with enough money to last through the winter.

Try, Try Again

Displaying the indefatigable spirit of a frontiersman, Charles planted wheat again in the spring. Unfortunately, the locusts had deposited eggs in the ground, and when the sun warmed the prairie, millions of green locusts pushed their way out. When the 1876 crops were ruined as well, Charles declared that he "just couldn't stay any longer in such a blasted country." So the family again loaded up its wagon and headed west. Over the next year, they spent time in Iowa and with relatives in South Troy, Minnesota.

Soon, Charles hastened a return to Walnut Grove. The family lived in town while Charles worked a variety of jobs: carpenter, store clerk, butcher, and miller. But in the winter of 1879, another calamity occurred. Laura's older sister, Mary, caught scarlet fever, and although Mary recovered, she gradually lost her eyesight until she was completely blind. Shortly thereafter, the Ingalls moved once more, this time to South Dakota.

Despite the hardships her family experienced in Minnesota, Laura had fond memories of her years there. In 1953, 74 years after her family left Walnut Grove, Laura wrote, "It was a lovely place, and I often think of it even yet and of the happy times I had playing along and in the creek."

Wild About Wilder

Today, Laura is honored by her Minnesota hometown. In 1995, the Laura Ingalls Wilder Historic Highway was established along Highway 14, from Lake Benton to Mankato. The highway passes through the town of Walnut Grove, where the Laura Ingalls Wilder Museum is located. The museum is an eight-building complex that features an 1898 depot, an 1880s school chapel, and an onion-domed house. Among the displays are a quilt Laura made by hand and a bible from the church Laura's family attended.

Every July, Walnut Grove holds the Wilder Pageant, a family-oriented outdoor drama based on Laura's life there. A hillside amphitheater on the banks of Plum Creek serves as the location of the live performances. Visitors can also go to the actual site of Laura's dugout home, though only a deep depression remains since the sod roof of the structure collapsed long ago and the walls have dissolved back into the creek.

To read about the Little House on the Prairie *television series, turn to page 101.*

DID YOU KNOW?

Although Laura Ingalls Wilder spent most of her adult life in Missouri, she and her husband lived in Spring Valley, Minnesota, from 1890 to 1891.

Fairly Good Art

Can art be made out of butter and seeds?

The Minnesota State Fair is one of summer's most popular events. Since it began, an estimated 50 million people have gone to the fair, and the all-time annual attendance record was 1,762,976 in 2001. People come for the rides, agriculture, and food (including many that are served "on a stick," a Minnesota tradition since the first Pronto Pup corn dog went on sale at the 1947 fair). And since 1965, the fair has offered two unique exhibits that draw big crowds: butter sculptures and crop art.

Princess Kay and the Butter

Since 1954, on the eve of the fair's opening day, 12 young ladies representing Minnesota's dairy-producing counties have competed for the title of Princess Kay of the Milky Way, the Minnesota dairy industry's goodwill ambassador. Princess Kay has many royal duties, but her first obligation is on the fair's opening day when she dons her crown and a winter jacket and crawls into a glass-enclosed, 38-degree revolving cooler. There, Princess Kay spends eight hours posing while fairgoers watch a sculptor render her head, neck, and shoulders from a 90-pound block of Grade A Minnesota butter.

Over the next 11 days, the other princess contestants take

turns posing in the revolving refrigerator. As the butter busts are completed, they go on display, and on the fair's closing day, each contestant takes home her buttery likeness as a souvenir.

Crop Art

For the fair's Crop Art and Arrangements competition, clever crafters use seeds, plant parts, glue, paint, and lacquer to create art. Entries have included everything from portraits of newsman Peter Jennings and former Minnesota governor Jesse Ventura to a replica of the state photograph *Grace*, showing corn dogs instead of gruel as the meal. The rules are pretty simple: all crop parts used must be from plants suited or adapted for growth in Minnesota. A best-in-show ribbon goes to the work judged to be the overall best creation in that year's competition.

Lillian Colton, a 94-year-old retired hairdresser from Owatonna, Minnesota, is one of the fair's crop art stars. Colton entered her first competition in 1966 and went on to win 11 Best of Show ribbons before she stopped competing. Over the years, her crop art creations have included likenesses of Bill Clinton, Shirley Temple, Billy Graham, Princess Diana, and the Northwestern National Bank building. Colton still shows her art at the fair and often provides demonstrations. In 2004, the Minneapolis Institute of the Arts displayed a special exhibition of Colton's work. The exhibit, titled *Lillian's Vision*, ran for two months and featured a mix of more than 50 pieces selected from Colton's personal collection. Now that's a fairly fantastic accomplishment!

Flour Power, Part II

*As C. C. Washburn built his flour empire near Saint Anthony Falls,
another transplanted New Englander with no milling experience was
carving out his own flour fiefdom across the Mississippi.*

While the Washburn mill flourished on the west side of the river, the situation on the east side wasn't so good. Flour mill after flour mill was failing. Their managers just didn't have the know-how or a superior product to keep them afloat. In 1869, three years after Washburn founded his mill, a New Hampshire native named Charles A. Pillsbury bought the east side's financially troubled Minneapolis Flour Mill and set about renovating it. Despite all evidence to the contrary, Pillsbury believed that the demand for Minnesota flour was great enough to support two major milling ventures. It was a gamble but one that paid off. The Pillsbury mill showed a profit in its first year of operation.

Barreling Along

With a profitable company came the desire to expand. By 1881, Charles Pillsbury had completed construction on a gigantic Pillsbury A-Mill, the largest in the world at that time.

The new Pillsbury A-Mill churned out flour faster than any other miller. When Pillsbury bought the failing Minneapolis

Flour Mill back in 1869, it was capable of producing 150 barrels of flour per day. By the time the A-Mill opened, the Pillsbury Company was producing 4,000 barrels per day at a time when other mills worldwide averaged about 500 barrels per day. Then, on October 12, 1882, the Pillsbury A-Mill set a record of 5,107 barrels of flour produced in a single day.

The X Games

Of course, the Pillsbury and Washburn companies competed for shares of the flour market. During the 1880s, while Washburn's company bragged about the medals its flour won, Pillsbury was staking out its own niche in the industry. Pillsbury had developed a process to refine and purify flour. Beginning in 1872, the company marked bags of its finest grade of flour with four Xs. Flour is graded according to its fineness, using a system of Xs. Until then, the finest grade of flour was classified XXX. So, when Pillsbury labeled his finest flour XXXX, he was announcing that his product was superior to any other, including Washburn's Gold Medal flour.

The Bake-Off

For the next half century, the companies battled for supremacy. Both offered an excellent product, so they sometimes turned to gimmicks to draw in consumers. In 1949, Pillsbury hit pay dirt.

That year, the Pillsbury Company held its first recipe contest. The contest took place at the Waldorf-Astoria hotel in New York City, and the goal was to see who could cook the best dish using Pillsbury baking products. Thousands of people entered that first year, and the winner was a Michigan woman named Theodora Smafield, who made no-knead, water-rising bread twists. She won $50,000.

The Pillsbury Bake-Off was so successful that the Pillsbury Company decided to make it a regular event. Today, the contest is held every other year and is as popular as ever. Entries since 1949 have included breads, cakes, pies, and even some main dishes, and the cash prize just keeps growing. The first million-dollar prize went to Kurt Wait in 1996. The Bake-Off has also spawned several cookbooks that promote the company's food products.

Pillsbury Goes to War

The Bake-Off didn't stop the competition between the two Minneapolis flour giants, but an earlier war had slowed it for a few years. World War II saw the companies working toward a common goal. While General Mills contributed technical products to the war effort, Pillsbury stayed closer to its product base. Its contributions remained food-related but were nevertheless of great use to the military. In particular, Pillsbury developed dehydrated soup mixes and innovative meal packaging so soldiers could be sure of fresh healthy meals even on the front lines. And as the Allies liberated Europe, Pillsbury products showed up on foreign tables and were even fed to prisoners of war.

The Urge to Merge

For more than 100 years, Pillsbury and General Mills competed for milling dominance in Minneapolis and around the world. It was a hard-fought battle between fierce competitors that offered the public similar, but not identical, products. In the end, both came out ahead. In 2002, the Pillsbury Company merged with General Mills, and the one-time Minnesota rivals became partners at last.

For the General Mills part of the story, turn to page 139.
To read about Pillsbury and General Mills
advertising icons, turn to page 266.

DID YOU KNOW?

The refrigerated dough the Pillsbury Doughboy represents has given rise to its own urban legend, widely circulated on the Internet. Although the details vary somewhat, the basic premise is always the same. According to the legend, a woman visiting her in-laws slumps over her steering wheel in a supermarket parking lot. Another shopper notices her and asks if she is OK. The woman says that she's been shot in the back of the head and has been holding in her brains for some time.

The good Samaritan calls the police, and when they arrive, they discover that a can of refrigerated dough in one of the shopping bags exploded from the heat inside the car. What the woman thinks is brain tissue is actually biscuit dough stuck to the back of her head.

Uncle John suspects that anyone buying this tale undoubtedly has mush for brains.

Haunted Happenings:
The Guthrie Theater

Next time you're taking in a performance of Hamlet *at the Guthrie Theater, remember that Richard Miller was once watching too.*

The Spook:
Richard Miller

What Happened?
On February 5, 1967, Richard Miller quit his usher's job at the Guthrie Theater in Minneapolis, bought a gun and ammunition at a local Sears store, went back to his car in the store's parking lot, and killed himself. He was wearing his Guthrie uniform when he died, and a suicide note found by police said he wanted to be buried in it.

A few weeks passed. Then one night, Guthrie patrons complained of an usher walking up and down Row 18 during a performance. They described him to managers as a gawky English teenager with a mole on his cheek. It couldn't be, could it? The description fit Richard Miller perfectly, and Row 18 had been one he'd patrolled.

After this first sighting, and for the next 25 years, people saw Miller everywhere. He rustled programs, paced Row 18, roamed the catwalks, and sat in the Queen's Box. Theater directors, actors, and janitors reported that pianos played by themselves and stage props moved of their own volition. Something had to be done.

The Exorcism

In 1993, fed up with the ghost's interference, theater managers called for an exorcism. Officially, they called it a "spiritual cleansing" and got a local Native American elder to perform it. What rituals the elder performed or techniques he used to rid the theater of its resident spook are unclear. But the cleansing seemed to work. A press representative from the theater reports, "Dick Miller's ghost hasn't been seen here since the early 1990s."

DID YOU KNOW?

A suspension bridge that linked Minneapolis to Nicollet Island opened in 1855 and was the first permanent span on the Mississippi River.

Party-Sota!

*Minnesotans are such a fun-loving bunch that they'll throw
a party for just about anything. Uncle John's got the skinny on
some of the state's most interesting festivals.*

The Aquatennial

Originally intended to celebrate water sports and aquatic activities, the Aquatennial in Minneapolis has morphed into an all-encompassing festival with many diverse events and activities. Minnesotans began this annual tradition in 1940 to salute summertime (something Minnesota has precious little of) and to foster a sense of civic pride. The celebration takes place every third week in July; the festival's founding fathers consulted weather forecasters to determine that this week was the warmest and driest of the year. At the celebration, revelers watch and participate in more than 70 events and competitions, including milk-carton boat races, a nighttime "Torchlight Parade" featuring illuminated floats, sandcastle competitions, beach parties, and the "Queen of the Lake" beauty pageant, where contestants from 49 Minnesota districts compete to become the Aquatennial queen.

The Fish House Parade

If you're visiting Aitken on the day after Thanksgiving, don't be surprised if you see somebody motoring down the street with a fish house in tow. That's because Aitken is the home of the Fish House Parade. Local store owners started the parade in 1990 to keep residents in town when they might otherwise leave for the long weekend to go shopping in the big cities. The plan worked, and today more than 6,000 people attend the annual event. The parade traditionally gets started with a pancake breakfast and ends with a dinner of Fish House stew. In between, entrants pull their fish houses through downtown Aitken. Past entries have included a brick fish house, one that sported a hot tub filled with girls in bikinis, and, Uncle John's favorite, a fish house pulled by a gas-powered commode.

The Burnsville Fire Muster

Every September, residents of Burnsville, Minnesota, put on a festival celebrating their fire department and firefighting services. The event began in 1980, when Roger Jackson, a local resident and fire equipment enthusiast, convinced local businesses that a fire muster would be a great idea for the community. They agreed, and the muster has been on fire ever since. The main attraction is a parade that showcases more than 100 classic and modern fire trucks and fire equipment gathered from around Minnesota and the Midwest. Local firefighters also put on firefighting demonstrations throughout the day.

Woodtick Racing

Every second Saturday in June, for more than 25 years, visitors to the Woodtick Inn at the Cuyuna Country State Recreation Area have been treated to a one-of-a-kind event: woodtick racing. The idea started in 1979 when the owner of the Cuyuna Bar (renamed the Woodtick Inn in 1984) and his friends picked some woodticks off of themselves and threw them into an ashtray to incinerate them. The ticks fled the bowl and raced across the table to get away from the burning embers. The next year, the organizers built a racetrack and organized the first race.

Don't have a tick? No problem. The folks at the Inn are happy to provide you with your own multi-legged steed. Personal tick owners be warned—these races are strictly regulated. The Inn's staff cheekily chide that they reserve the right to randomly check your tick for illegal steroids, so no funny stuff. The race organizers also stick to a strict schedule of "jockey" meetings at noon and the actual race starting at one o'clock.

DID YOU KNOW?

Minnesota's magnificent North Country pine forests formed during the Mesozoic era, 70 to 225 million years ago.

Minnesota Curio, Part II

Our list of Minnesota's interesting attractions continues.
(Part I begins on page 75.)

The Two-Story Outhouse, Belle Plaine

Get a load of this: In Belle Plaine, Minnesota, attached to the historic Hooper-Bowler-Hillstrom house (now a museum), is one of the country's only two-story outhouses. Other states claim the first or the largest or the only one made of brick, and these claims may or may not be true; we've heard a rumor that the two-story loo in Arkansas may be a sham! But what we do know for certain is that, in Minnesota, this john's the real thing. In the 1880s, the Bowler family moved into the farmhouse and realized they needed more room. The Bowlers were a large family of 13, and a single outhouse just wouldn't do. So the patriarch, Samuel Bowler, constructed a double-deck privy to keep down the whines about too-long lines. There are five . . . ahem . . . thrones in the outhouse. Now that's ingenuity.

World's Largest Turkey Roast, Frazee

There are no official records to examine for this one, but we believe the world's largest turkey roast took place in Frazee, Minnesota, on July 1, 1998. By "world's largest," we mean the roasting of the largest turkey, a 22-foot tall fiberglass bird named Big Tom. As maintenance crews gave Tom a spruce-up for that year's Turkey Days Festival, a blowtorch lit Tom's leg, and the bird went up in flames. It was all a gobbling mess, as you can imagine. Fire trucks from neighboring towns rushed to the scene, but Tom couldn't be saved. So on September 19, 1998, 22-foot-tall Big Tom II took his place as Frazee's turkey mascot, and the town's maintenance crews were taught to be a little more careful with their torches.

World's Largest Foot, Vining

At the entrance to the town of Vining stands the world's largest foot and swollen toe. The sculpture is the creation of former construction worker, now artist, Ken Nyberg. The foot and toe are made of steel, weigh 1,200 pounds, and stand 11 feet tall. Of his inspiration for the statue, Nyberg says only that he wanted to create something that didn't have a person in it. He succeeded, though the toe often has a person on it, as the sculpture has become a favorite photo spot for tourists.

Want to see other Nyberg art "by-the-road"? Vining is a bit like an outdoor Nyberg museum. He has creations on display all over town, including a pair of pliers crushing a bug, a giant clothespin, and a cup of coffee mysteriously spilling its contents.

The Bunyans

Although other states also call Paul Bunyan a native, Minnesota considers itself his "real" birthplace and offers up enormous Bunyan statues and accessories as proof.

Talking Paul, Brainerd

For years touted as the world's largest animated man, a talking statue of Paul Bunyan at the entrance to the Paul Bunyan Amusement Center in Brainerd greeted visitors by name. In 1949, the Chicago Northwestern Railroad built talking Paul to commemorate its lumber business. A year later, the railroad sold the statue to the amusement center (then called Paul Bunyan Land). Paul stands (er . . . sits) 26 feet high, has a 150-inch waist, and a size-80 neck. In 2003, the amusement center closed, and Paul moved to another theme park called This Old Farm's Pioneer Village located just outside town.

Paul's Lady Friend, Hackensack

Not willing to be outdone, the people of Hackensack decided that Paul Bunyan needed a girlfriend. Spending all those chilly nights alone in the woods made him an unhappy fellow. So in 1952, a Hackensack man built Paul a sweetheart. Named Lucette Diana Kensack, she's a pleasant young lady with a perpetual smile, a blue-and-white striped skirt, and a red blouse. Lucette is quite the giant herself and stands 17 feet tall—a big girl, no doubt, but certainly still a dainty match for Brainerd's talking Paul.

DID YOU KNOW?

The Native American groups indigenous to Minnesota are the Anishinabe (also called the Ojibwa) and the Dakota.

All Agape for Agates

*What's really old, has bright red, orange, and yellow designs,
and ranges in size from teeny-tiny to bowling-ball big? Just ask
the folks from Moose Lake, Minnesota, and they'll tell
you: the Lake Superior agate, that's what.*

More than one billion years ago, North America split apart,
leaving a large valley in what is now the area covered by
Lake Superior. Hot lava filled the basin and trapped water
vapor and carbon dioxide gas bubbles inside. Water passed
through these gas-filled pockets and left behind silica mineral
deposits like quartz and chalcedony. As the lava cooled, the
gases and minerals hardened into the stones we now call Lake
Superior agates.

A Little Recognition Would Be Nice

For the most part, the stones remained trapped in the lava
flows until the Ice Age began and a large piece of glacial ice,
known as the Superior lobe (which eventually melted and
filled many of Minnesota's lakes and rivers), made its way
though Minnesota. As the glacial ice traveled southward
between 10,000 and 15,000 years ago, it carried the agates
along for the ride. Between the glacier's movement and
constant cycle of freezing and thawing, the ancient stones
were fractured and polished before finally being deposited

throughout the northeastern and north-central parts of the state.

In 1969, at the urging of agate aficionado and Minnesotan Jean Dahlberg, the state legislature declared the agate the state gemstone. There were other choices: pipestone (a stone Native Americans used to craft peace pipes) and red, iron-rich bing-hamite were among the other entries. But in the end, the legislature decided that the agate's geological birth most closely mirrored that of the state and thus made it the perfect choice.

The Big Stampede

Today, a Lake Superior agate is a prized find for many Minnesotans; agates are beautiful, and they are the state gemstone, after all. But collectors no longer need to wander lakeshores and riverbanks hoping to stumble upon a stone. They need only to visit the town of Moose Lake, the self-proclaimed "Agate Capital of the World," and home to the world's largest agate, a 108-pound rock on display at the First National Bank. The town also hosts an Agate Days Festival every July, during which a driver dumps a truckload of rock mixed with agates and quarters in the middle of Main Street. "The Big Stampede," as the event is called, starts off with a shotgun's BANG, and then the crowd scrambles for the hidden treasures. May the best agate lover win!

DID YOU KNOW?

The 643-acre Quarry Park and Nature Reserve in Saint Cloud was once a successful granite quarry. Today, its man-made craggy cliffs are a haven for hikers and skiers looking for steep slopes on the otherwise flat prairie.

Tonka Toys

To many, Tonka trucks represent what is best about America.
They're tough, strong, and long-lasting. And they have
their roots firmly planted in Minnesota.

The Background

In the 1940s, three Minnesotans (Lynn Baker, Avery Crounse, and Alvin Tesch) decided to start a garden tool manufacturing company in the basement of a local school. They called it the Mound Metalcraft Company, after their suburban Minneapolis hometown.

Toy manufacturer L. E. Streater Industries was just up the road from Mound Metalcraft. And since this was a small Minnesota town where everybody knew everybody else, there was frequent contact between the companies. Edward C. Streater approached the folks at Mound and offered them a deal. He'd give them a design for a metal toy steam shovel and the tools to produce it if they'd help him sell the tools. For Streater, it was a way to drum up business. For the Mound people, toys seemed more interesting than garden tools, and they jumped at the chance. In 1947, Mound came out with its first models: the #100 Steam Shovel and #150 Crane and Clam. Both debuted at the 1947 New York toy show.

The Mound group branded the toys "Tonka" after nearby Lake Minnetonka. In the Sioux language, the word *tonka* means "great," and the name proved prophetic for the company. In its first year, Tonka produced 37,000 toy shovels and cranes, and they sold out in only a few months.

In the mid-1950s, Mound Metalcraft became Tonka Toys, and manufacturing continued in Minnesota until 1983. In 1991, toy manufacturing giant Hasbro acquired Tonka Toys and continues to sell the Tonka brand.

Since its inception, Tonka has produced more than 30 models of trucks and vehicles. Each year, the company uses 5.1 million pounds of sheet metal and 119,000 pounds of yellow paint to make its toys.

The Mighty Dump

In 1965, Tonka released what became its most popular model: the Mighty Dump Truck. To advertise the toy, commercials depicted a fully grown elephant standing on the truck, a graphic demonstration of its indestructibility. The toy weighed less than five pounds; the elephant weighed six tons.
Kids and their parents couldn't get enough of the Mighty Dump Truck. Sales soared, and by the 1990s, Tonka was making between 900,000 and one million dump trucks every year.

Life Imitates Toy

Kids aren't the only ones who have taken notice of durable Tonka trucks. Even Detroit came calling. Recognizing the quality of the Tonka brand, the Ford Motor Company teamed with Tonka designers to develop a real truck that incorporated some of the toy's features. Unveiled at the 2002 Detroit auto show, Ford's F-350 Mighty Tonka was a concept vehicle for new Ford pickups; it wasn't for sale, but it did use the Tonka name to bring attention to Ford's trucks.

Fun Fact:

Several military-style Tonka toy vehicles manufactured in 1964 bore the serial number GR2-2431, the telephone number of the Mound Tonka plant.

DID YOU KNOW?

Minnesota is the birthplace of modern cheerleading. In 1898, Gopher fan Johnny Campbell couldn't contain his emotions during a University of Minnesota football game. His team was losing, and in an effort to urge them on, Johnny began chanting

Rah, Rah, Rah!

Sku-u-mah, Hoo-rah, Hoo-rah!

Varsity, Varsity!

Minn-e-so-tah!

Soon the crowd around him was on its feet chanting along. The team was inspired too, and Minnesota won the game. Johnny's enthusiastic cheer spread to other schools, which adapted it to their own teams.

Birth of a Team

*Minnesota's Major League Baseball franchise has grown into
a successful team, but its birth was fraught with difficulty.*

Strike One

The popularity of baseball exploded in the years immediately
after the Civil War, and Minnesota got in on the craze. Minor
leagues sprouted up all over the state. Many folded as quickly
as they came, but in 1884, one tenacious team from Saint Paul
was determined to finish out the season. The Saint Paul
Baseball Club outlived its bankrupt minor league by jumping
to a newly formed major one: the Union Association. The team
played nine games that year but won only two, placing ninth
out of 12 Union Association teams.

The next year, the Union Association dissolved, and the city
of Saint Paul lost its team. But one thing remained in the city:
the distinction of having had Minnesota's first major league baseball team. Saint Paul residents had tasted big-league glory, and
they set their sights on finding another team and keeping it.

Strike Two

The citizens of Minnesota clamored for more baseball, and
soon two minor-league teams, the Minneapolis Millers and the
Saint Paul Saints, were competing in the Western League,

another upstart minor organization. Western creator Ban Johnson, a sportswriter from Ohio, hoped that his Western League would soon rival the major National League.

The Millers excelled in the Western League, racking up impressive stats. The team's original home field, called Athletic Park, was small, making it easier to post impressive numbers, but the Millers' success cannot be attributed only to that. In 1894, Perry "Moose" Werden hit a record 42 home runs and then slugged 45 the next year, a feat unmatched until Babe Ruth began to work his magic. The Millers also won the Western League flag (like the pennant) in 1896, giving Minneapolis its first professional baseball championship.

The Saint Paul Saints played their first game in 1895 at a small ballpark in Saint Paul. The team also gained local fans, but in 1900, owner Charles Comiskey decided the team would be better off playing in Chicago. There they remain, now known as the Chicago White Sox.

Foul Ball

In 1901, Ban Johnson saw his vision realized. His Western League became the major American League, a rival to the National. Despite their successes, the Millers were one of four teams dropped when the league turned major.

The Millers and a reconstituted Saints team continued to play successful minor-league baseball for 59 years. But the minors weren't good enough for the twin cities of Saint Paul and Minneapolis. They were itching for another chance at the majors. That chance finally came from, believe it or not, the American League.

Home Run!

The poor, poor Washington Senators. They were one of the oldest franchises in organized baseball, created in 1859 as an amateur team to play the Potomacs, a team made up mainly of government clerks. For most of their long history, the Senators were the underdogs. They didn't win very often, and their inability to succeed even became the team's unofficial motto: "First in war, first in peace, and last in the American League." A World Series title in 1924 and three American League championships could not combat their reputation. Game attendance was dropping, and so was the team's hope for the future.

In 1960, team president Calvin Griffith began scouting for the Senators' new home. His search quickly turned to Minneapolis, which had built a new stadium a few years earlier with the hope of luring a professional team. The Washington Senators became the Minnesota Twins, and the newly named team played its first game on April 11, 1961, against the defending American League champion New York Yankees. In a surprising twist, the Twins beat the Yankees at Yankee Stadium 6–0. The rest is history:

- Twins' World Series championships: two (1987, 1991)
- American League championships: three (1965, 1987, 1991)
- Hall of Famers: six (Rod Carew, Steve Carlton, Harmon Killebrew, Paul Molitor, Kirby Puckett, Dave Winfield)
- Retired Numbers: five (#3 Harmon Killebrew, #6 Tony Oliva, #14 Kent Hrbek, #29 Rod Carew, #34 Kirby Puckett)

Fun Facts About Minnesota Baseball:

- The Saints and Millers weren't the only professional baseball teams in Minnesota before the arrival of the Twins. In 1944, the Minneapolis Millerettes played for one season in the All-American Girls Professional Baseball League, the subject of the movie *A League of Their Own*. Halfway through the season, poor attendance at home forced the Millerettes to change their schedule and play the rest of their games on the road. The team never caught on with Minnesotans, and the Millerettes moved to Fort Wayne, Indiana, playing as the Fort Wayne Daisies the next year.

- Although no official Negro League team ever played for Minnesota, the state does have a connection to the league's inception. Andrew "Rube" Foster was an occasional pitcher for the all-black Saint Paul Gophers before he went on to create the Negro League.

- In the early 1900s, while playing in a hotly contested (and muddy) game against the Saint Paul Saints, Andy Oyler of the Minneapolis Millers hit a 24-inch home run. While trying to duck from a fast pitch, he accidentally made contact with the ball, but no one saw where it went. While he sped around the bases, the second baseman for the Saints gave chase, thinking that Oyler was hiding the ball in his pocket. It wasn't until Oyler had rounded the bases that the mystery was solved: the ball had been driven into the mud two feet in front of home plate. Score!

Minnesota Movie Madness

*Despite weather extremes that make shooting a film a challenge,
Minnesota is the setting for a surprising number of movies.
Here are some of the most memorable.*

Fargo (1996)

By far, the film that best captures Minnesota's personality is
Fargo. Set primarily in the fictional (but based on the real)
town of Brainerd, all the characters in this movie speak with an
unmistakable Minnesota accent, and the dialogue abounds
with phrases like "you betcha" and "you're durn tootin'." A
murder has taken place on the outskirts of town, and it's up to
Brainerd's pregnant sheriff, Marge (played by Frances
McDormand), to solve the crime. The plot winds its way
through unexpected and increasingly absurd outcomes as inept
criminals commit bungled crimes.

Fargo Facts:

- *Fargo* was written, directed, and produced by Joel and Ethan
  Coen, brothers who were born in Saint Louis Park and
  Minneapolis, respectively.
- The shooting schedule for the film had to be changed multi-
  ple times because spring was coming and the snow kept
  melting. In the end, the movie's setting is a compilation of

locations in Minnesota, North Dakota, and Canada.

- The seal for Marge's Brainerd police department features a picture of Paul Bunyan and Babe the Blue Ox.
- William H. Macy's character, Jerry Lundegaard, shares his last name with movie critic Bob Lundegaard, who wrote for the *Minneapolis Star and Tribune* from 1973 to 1986.
- The car dealership featured in the movie was in Richfield, Minnesota. It no longer exists; the spot is now home to Best Buy's corporate headquarters.
- *Fargo* won two Academy Awards: Frances McDormand won for best actress, and Joel and Ethan Coen won for best original screenplay.
- Joel Coen and Frances McDormand have been married since 1984.

Purple Rain (1984)

Minneapolis native Prince used this movie to portray the raw and raunchy Minneapolis nightclub scene. In fact, the film's principal setting, the First Avenue Club, is a real Minneapolis nightclub that's still in operation; parts of *Purple Rain* were shot there.

Filmed almost entirely at night, *Purple Rain* tells the story of a musician called "the Kid" (Prince). Although full of talent and promise, he struggles to meet expectations while battling his inner demons. Soon, a beautiful singer named Apollonia (Apollonia Kotero) arrives looking for her big break, and the Kid's world is shaken. One of the film's most memorable scenes occurs when the Kid takes Apollonia for a ride on his purple motorcycle. When they arrive at a deserted lakeshore, the Kid says she must "purify" herself in the waters of Lake Minnetonka. Apollonia strips and jumps into the icy water without hesitation, but when she emerges, the Kid informs her that this isn't Lake Minnetonka. Prince won an Academy Award for *Purple Rain,* though for its musical score rather than his acting.

Grumpy Old Men (1993)

Written by Hastings native Mark Steven Johnson, *Grumpy Old Men* is almost a travelogue depicting winter in Minnesota. From the irony of the opening credits—shots of a snowplow plodding down the street, blocking in the cars parked at the curb, while "Heat Wave" croons over the soundtrack—we know that we are about to get a taste of life in the frozen North.

The setting is Wabasha, Minnesota. Six inches of snow are on the ground, and it isn't even Thanksgiving yet. The grumpy old men, John Gustafson (Jack Lemmon) and his nemesis Max Goldman (Walter Matthau), spend a good part of each day digging their cars out of snowbanks and trading barbs and epithets as they work.

The big excitement in men's lives, before the appearance of a glamorous and quirky new neighbor (Ann-Margret), is ice fishing on a nearby lake where they have adjoining shanties. Before the movie is finished, audiences will have witnessed people slipping on the ice, people being buried in snow falling from a roof, people riding snowmobiles in the middle of the night, and an ice-fishing shack falling through thin ice.

Drop Dead Gorgeous (1999)

What the Texas cheerleader's murdering mom did for Texas and, well, cheerleading, *Drop Dead Gorgeous* did for Minnesota and beauty pageants. Written by Lona Williams, the film portrays quirky Middle American life and customs. Williams's hometown of Rosemount, Minnesota, has been transformed into Mount Rose, home of "the oldest living Lutheran" (recently deceased). It's a town where beauty pageants are serious business, where teenagers practice their "talents" and dream of winning as a way out. It's a town where parents push their children to conform, where middle-aged men take prurient interest in the nubile contestants, and where most mothers seem to be former beauty contest winners themselves. The reigning Teen Princess is an anorexic who spends her days in an eating disorder rehab center. And everyone smokes.

Amber Atkins (Kirsten Dunst), a good-hearted girl from a trailer park, dreams of following in the footsteps of her idol, Diane Sawyer (1963's Junior Miss). Amber practices her talent (tap dancing) while she applies makeup to cadavers at the local mortuary, her after-school job. The 50th anniversary commemorative pageant for the American Teen Princess title is coming up, and Amber is the only one who seems to represent a measure of competition for the town's richest spoiled girl, Rebecca "Becky" Leeman (Denise Richards), who is expected to win. But as the pageant preparations progress, the death toll begins to mount.

Spam Town USA

I scream, you scream, we all scream for Spam!

Town: Austin
Location: Mower County
Founding: 1854
Current population: 23,000
Size: 10.8 square miles
Median age: 39.7 years
County seat: Yes

What's in a Name?
Austin gets its name from trapper Austin Nichols, who came to the area in 1853. Nichols stopped near the Cedar River, built a log cabin, staked his claim, and the town was born.

Claims to Fame:
- Austin is first and foremost the birthplace of Spam. In 1891, George A. Hormel, a butcher, founded Hormel and Company in an abandoned creamery about one-half mile outside the town.
- Hormel's mansion still stands in town. Built in 1871, the house originally was home to Austin's then-mayor John Cook. Hormel bought it in 1901 and began renovations the

next year. He added many features, including front columns imported from Italy and stained-glass windows.

- In September 2001, the Spam Museum opened in Austin. There, visitors can view, among other things, the "wall of Spam" (a wall constructed of thousands of Spam cans) and the interactive Spam cyber café. The museum also holds an annual Spam Jam, what they call a "Spamily reunion," that includes celebrity appearances, musical events, and food offerings ranging from Spam-and-eggs to Spam burgers.
- There is more to Austin than Spam. OK, not a lot more. But the town was home to the Cedar River's first sawmill. Homesteader Chauncey Leverich built the mill between the years 1854 and 1855.

To read more about Spam, turn to page 212.

DID YOU KNOW?

In the early 1920s, the Pendergast Candy Company in Minneapolis accidentally invented fluffy nougat. The company produced a chocolate-covered, hard nougat bar called the "Emma." But one day, candy makers added too many eggs to a mixture of nougat, and it expanded into the fluffy, soft sweet we know today. Pendergast execs decided to add the soft nougat to their candy bars anyway and changed the name to "Fat Emma." Soon after, an independent candy maker named Frank Mars (from Newport, Minnesota) borrowed Pendergast's recipe and incorporated it into the Milky Way bar, first sold in 1923. Mars later also added fluffy nougat to Snickers and Mars bars.

Famous Minnesotans

Why is this face smiling? He's proudly bearing the names of 33 people with strong ties to the North Star State. They were born there, grew up there, or maybe played ball for a Minnesota team. They're comedians, writers, politicians, singers, actors, artists, models, and athletes. How many can you find?

LONI ANDERSON

RICHARD DEAN ANDERSON

JAMES ARNESS

JESSICA BIEL

WARREN BURGER

ROD CAREW

RACHEL LEIGH COOK

BOB DYLAN

MIKE FARRELL

F. SCOTT FITZGERALD

AL FRANKEN

JUDY GARLAND

J. PAUL GETTY

JOSH HARTNETT

GARRISON KEILLOR

JESSICA LANGE

SINCLAIR LEWIS

JOHN MADDEN

ROGER MARIS

E.G. MARSHALL

LEROY NEIMAN

PRINCE

MARION ROSS

JANE RUSSELL

WINONA RYDER

CHARLES SCHULZ

KEVIN SORBO

LEA THOMPSON

CHERYL TIEGS

ANNE TYLER

DEWITT WALLACE

DAVE WINFIELD

JESSE VENTURA

```
                  R Q J L
                W S Y I A R O F M B
            T E I T M C J C L S E A O E
          C R R T I V H H Q H O H U R B Q
        U A A E K U L A E A L E N H R I D P
      S C M G E L E I R C D R C L I A J O Y P
    M D R L F M C Y T D S W N L V L A R D N L T
    O E U A P N G Q T D J E S S E V E N T U R A
  R G A R R I S O N K E I L L O R S R I D N R O N
  O P R S R H Q       A N B L       S W G E E N S
  R J E I P E E Q     N V N G       C C T H R T G S
  W L O N G V H K     A G I A       Q F H O C S T W
Q L S I W E L R I A L C N I S H T N R T R C U C O O V Z
E C A L L A W T T I W E D D A V E W I N F I E L D O N E
Z F S C O T T F I T Z G E R A L D F N P O P S P Z S K C
P W A R R E N B U R G E R       N O S P M O H T A E L H J
U N M I       U M J E S S I C A L A N G E     C E A G
  G E W F     Q W I N O N A R Y D E R       D R N U
  P K D M A   N E K N A R F L A K         F Y E X O
  E N D V E                             G L R W L
  Y W K A A T                         O T U Q F C
  K N A M I E N Y O R E L E I B A C I S S E J
  A L X N V Z H J A M E S A R N E S S P X X
  D T L N H J L L A H S R A M G E A Y N K
    O B R O S N I V E K N S L Q S M A
      J E B J U D Y G A R L A N D
```

For answers, turn to page 309.

Respect the Law

Minnesotans get themselves into all kinds of legal trouble, a lot of it downright silly. To make our case, we present the following.

Spoiled Safari

During an African safari in 2000, Scottish lion hunter Rolf Rohwer confronted a charging lion and shot it at close range. The lion continued charging, however, and ultimately mauled Rohwer before it died of its wounds. After recovering from his own injuries, Rohwer sued the Federal Cartridge Company of Anoka, Minnesota; the company had manufactured the bullet Rohwer used on the lion. Rohwer claimed the company failed to properly label the bullets with a warning that they wouldn't stop a charging lion at close range. The case did go to trial but was dismissed in December 2004; a lionhearted Minnesota judge ruled that the evidence Rohwer presented to validate his claim was spurious and that the bullet manufacturer could not be held liable.

Unhappy Trails

In March 2001, 72-year-old Fritz Herring of Edina went to the Hennepin County Government Center in Minneapolis to deliver a singing telegram to a country-and-western fan who worked there. Instead, he ended up in a heap of trouble.

Dressed as a cowboy and packing an imitation .44 caliber pistol in his gun belt, Herring moseyed into the lobby, only to be told to "put 'em up" by a sheriff's deputy spooked by the gun. Herring explained who he was and even produced written proof of his assignment, but it didn't matter. The deputy arrested him, and Herring sat in jail for 12 hours before he was released.

Keep Your Pants On!

Apparently, waiting in line during the security screening process at Minneapolis–Saint Paul's International Airport proved to be a bit too much for passenger Darryl Miller. In July 2004, screeners selected Miller for a random security search. When a screener passed a wand over the front of his body, Miller dropped his pants, and he wasn't wearing any underwear! As you can imagine, this was more than the screeners had been hoping to find, and they quickly called security officers, who arrested Miller for indecent exposure.

DID YOU KNOW?

The Mississippi River isn't the only major waterway with its source in Minnesota. Both the Red River of the North and Saint Lawrence River begin in the state.

School Daze:
Sports Rivalries

Sports are an important part of life for many Minnesota college students, and where there are sports, of course, there are rivalries.

The University of Minnesota: The Little Brown Jug

One of the most well-known rivalries exists between the University of Minnesota Gophers and the University of Michigan Wolverines and involves the Little Brown Jug. The story begins in 1903, when the Gophers football team hosted the Wolverines. That year's Minnesota team was one of the best in the school's history, but Michigan had been unbeaten for 28 straight games.

The game was close, and the Gophers kept the Wolverines from racking up their usual big score. But Michigan was winning throughout the first half and into the second. Then, late in the second half, Minnesota scored to tie the game 6–6. Pandemonium broke out as Minnesota fans stormed the field in celebration. There was so much chaos that, even though two minutes remained, referees called the game and declared it a tie.

The Wolverines went back to Michigan but left behind their five-gallon, stoneware water jug. The next day, Minnesota custodian Oscar Munson found it (some have hinted that he may have pinched it from Michigan coach Fielding Yost out of spite, but that's never been proved). Munson brought the jug to L. J. Cooke, head of Minnesota's athletics department. The custodian spoke with a heavy Scandinavian accent, and his words, as he handed the jug to Cooke, have become part of Minnesota lore: "Jost left his yug," he announced.

Cooke and Munson decided to decorate the jug. On its side, they wrote, "Michigan jug—captured by Oscar, October 31, 1903." They also recorded the game's score: "Michigan 6, Minnesota 6." Minnesota's score was written many times larger than Michigan's.

Soon after, Yost decided he wanted the jug back. When he asked for it, Cooke replied, "We have your little brown jug; if you want it, you'll have to win it." And so the rivalry was born. Michigan won back the jug the next time the teams met in 1909. Then, in 1920, both sides decided to give the jug a glossy brown paint job and name it the "Little Brown Jug."

Over the last century, the jug has been up for grabs each time the two schools compete. League schedules vary from year to year, so the matchups haven't been annual, but there have been 83 games in all. Michigan has won 59, Minnesota 21, and three games were tied. Minnesota beat Michigan 23–20 in Ann Arbor at the 2005 match-up. Team officials record the results of every game on the jug, and the trophy remains at the winner's campus until the next time the schools battle it out on the gridiron.

Saint Olaf vs. Carleton: Getting the Goat

Saint Olaf and Carleton are two small liberal arts colleges at opposite ends of Northfield, Minnesota, so it's reasonable that a sports rivalry grew between them. In fact, the rivalry between the schools is more than 100 years old, making it one of the oldest in collegiate sports history. What's unexpected is the tradition the pair devised to reward winners.

A fierce competition between the two teams determines the winner of a much sought-after trophy: a wooden goat. The tradition started in 1913 at a basketball game. Endre Anderson, a Saint Olaf student, was looking for a way to "get the goat" of his school's rival. He decided to carve a small wooden goat and hang it from the gym's rafters during the game. Saint Olaf lost, however, so the Carleton players took the goat figure down and brought it back to their campus as a trophy. Thus, the tradition began. In order to claim the goat trophy for the year, a school must sweep the other in both basketball and football. If they split the events, the trophy's possessor keeps it for another year.

For college traditions, turn to page 39.

DID YOU KNOW?

Saint Olaf College's fight song (entitled "Um Ya Ya") is one of only a few college songs to directly mention another school in its lyrics—that school being Carleton, of course. The tune goes as follows:

> We come from Saint Olaf, we sure are the real stuff.
> Our team is the cream of the colleges great.
> We fight fast and furious, our team is injurious.
> Tonight Carleton College will sure meet its fate.

The Great Hinckley Fire

On September 1, 1894, one of the worst fires
in American history engulfed Hinckley, Minnesota.

Before the fire, Hinckley was a prospering town of about
1,200. Abundant white pine trees had been attracting log-
gers to the area since the 1860s, and the town grew up around
the logging industry.

The Fire

September 1, 1894, was unusually hot and dry in Hinckley.
Between May and September, the area got only two inches of
rain, and temperatures consistently reached the mid-90s. Yet
trains continued to run even though cinders from their smoke-
stacks posed a fire hazard. And lumberjacks continued to light
small fires to clear areas where they worked.

On September 1, two of the small fires merged into a
firestorm. The blaze produced winds that swirled at 80 mph,
and just outside the town, flames and heat were consuming the
railroad ties. By the time the firestorm blew into Hinckley
around 3:30 P.M., its flames were four miles high and it had
reached a temperature of 1,000 degrees.

The fire burned for four hours and destroyed 350,000 acres
in Minnesota and Wisconsin. Four hundred people died in the

Hinckley area alone, and reports of the fire showed up in newspapers as far away as New York. Many of those stories included tales of heroic Minnesotans and the several hundred people they saved.

The Engineers

As the fire burned, two northbound trains approached Hinckley: a freight train, driven by Edward Barry, and a passenger train, driven by Edward Best. Barry arrived first; Best pulled in a few minutes later. Faced with the raging fire and hundreds of townspeople running toward them to escape the blaze, the men decided to connect the three boxcars on Best's train to the five coaches on Barry's in order to make one long train that could whisk fleeing townspeople away from danger.

The engineers loaded passengers onto the train and rolled out of town. About 10 miles north of Hinckley, they reached a bridge 150 feet above the rushing waters of the Kettle River. The bridge was the only way to get away from the fire, but the structure had already started to burn. Barry and Best knew they had to cross the bridge or they would be trapped between the fire and the gorge. So they continued on, even as the bridge burned. They made it safely across, but the train cleared the bridge by only 2,000 feet before the structure collapsed into the river.

The Third Train

While the two Edwards and their crews were escaping north, a third train was headed for Hinckley on its way to Saint Paul. The train, engineered by Jim Root, carried 150 passengers.

About a mile outside Hinckley, Root saw townspeople

racing toward his train. They begged him to let them on, and he stopped just long enough for them to jump aboard. Root picked up more than 150 people and headed away from town. On the way, the baggage car and fuel car caught fire. A quick-thinking porter doused the flames with a fire extinguisher as windows exploded around him. Root just kept driving until he reached a small body of water called Skunk Lake, 18 inches deep and about five miles outside town. There, he and his 300 passengers got off the train and huddled in the muddy water for four hours until rain started to fall and the fire died down. The brush and trees around them burned to the ground, but only three of Root's passengers died.

The Gravel Pit

In Hinckley, hundreds of people were trapped as the firestorm surrounded the town, and fire chief John Craig knew he had to do something. There was a gravel pit in the middle of town that Eastern Minnesota Railroad workers had dug in preparation for laying a railroad track. The pit was about three acres wide, 30 feet deep, and often full of water. Most of the water had evaporated during the drought, but three feet remained. It was enough.

Craig mounted his horse and rode through town, directing people to the gravel pit. His plan was successful. All 100 people (and many animals) who plunged into the water survived.

On the Lake

Just outside Hinckley, in a cabin on Grindstone Lake, lived the Patrick family. One of the children, Frank Patrick, later spoke of his rescue from the Hinckley fire. As the fire approached his family's cabin, his mother loaded him, his brother, and herself into a boat and pushed off onto the lake. As they drifted and shouted for help, the flames around them licked the sides of their boat, and the vessel caught fire.

Through the thick smoke came an Ojibwa woman in a canoe. She loaded Frank and his family into her canoe and took them back to her house where she cared for them until the fire died down and it was safe for them to return home.

Hinckley Today

There wasn't much to return to, however. The Great Hinckley Fire destroyed the town, its surroundings, and the pine forests that had supported its economy. Many people believed Hinckley would never again amount to anything more than a dusty prairie railroad crossing. In fact, a *New York Times* columnist wrote just after the fire, "There is little probability of Hinckley ever being rebuilt to its former prosperous proportions."

The statement was prophetic. In November 1894, just two months after the fire, the Northern Pacific Railroad rebuilt Hinckley's train depot, hoping the town would be reborn as a railroad crossing. That didn't happen, and it was almost a century before Hinckley showed any real signs of life. In the 1990s, construction of the Grand Casino revived the town's economy. Today, in addition to the casino, Hinckley has several prosperous businesses and a permanent population of about 1,200.

Hinckley also boasts the Hinckley Fire Museum. Located in the old train depot (the one Northern Pacific rebuilt after the fire), the museum tells the story of the town, the fire, and its aftermath. The museum has been open since 1976.

The Timberwolves by the Numbers

NBA basketball has always belonged in Minnesota. It just took a few years to convince the league. Almost 30 years after the Lakers left for Los Angeles, the NBA finally returned to the Twin Cities in 1989 in the form of the Timberwolves.

1

Numbers retired by the Timberwolves (#2 Malik Sealey)

2

Stadiums the Timberwolves have called home. The franchise played its first season at the Metrodome but moved to the Target Center in 1990.

3

Timberwolves selected to the NBA All-Star game (Kevin Garnett, 1997–1998, 2000–2006; Tom Gugliotta, 1997; Wally Szczerbiak, 2002)

4

Pick with which the Timberwolves nabbed Georgia Tech point guard Stephon Marbury in the 1996 NBA draft; and 50-win seasons in franchise history (2000, 2002–2004)

6

Number of times Kevin Garnett has been named to the NBA
All-Defensive first team (2000–2005)

7

Head coaches in franchise history (Bill Musselman, Jimmy
Rodgers, Sidney Lowe, Bill Blair, Flip Saunders, Kevin McHale,
Dwayne Casey)

8

Consecutive playoff appearances by the Timberwolves
(1997–2004)

9

Number of times Kevin Garnett has been named to the NBA
All-Star team (1997–1998, 2000–2006)

22

Games won by the Timberwolves during their 1989–1990 inau-
gural season

50

Different costumes the Timberwolves Dance Team uses in one
season

101.3

Jersey number of the Timberwolves' mascot, Crunch

338

Fouls committed by forward Sam Mitchell during the 1991 season, the most in the league that year

734

Assists dished out by point guard Pooh Richardson during the 1991 season, his second year in the league

49,551

Fans who attended the Timberwolves' final game at the Metrodome on April 17, 1990. The turnout was the third largest in NBA history.

DID YOU KNOW?

The Metrodome was demolished in 1995, but it was tough to destroy. After the first explosives detonated, most of the building was still standing. The demolition crew had to bring in a wrecking ball and knock down the arena by hand.

Minnesotisms: Weather and Geography

Uncle John's lesson in speaking Minnesotan continues.

The Weather

Here's all you need to know to carry on a conversation about the weather any time of the year.

Subject: Winter
Possible Conversation: Cold enough for you?
Ya, she's a cold one, but it's not the cold so much as the wind-chill that really gets to a guy.

Subject: Spring
Possible Conversation: Nice weather for a change.
Ya, but it won't be long before it's hotter than heck.

Subject: Summer
Possible Conversation: Hot enough for you?
She's a hot one, but it's not the heat so much as the humidity that really gets to a guy.

Subject: Fall
Possible Conversation: Nice weather for a change.
Ya, but it won't be long before the snow flies.

Geography

Minnesotans like their state, and they have special terms for its geography. Here's all you need to know to get around.

The Cabin

What Minnesotans call a summer home, usually located on a lake

The Lake

What Minnesotans call the body of water located nearest to their cabins

Up North

Any place north of the Twin Cities

Down South

Iowa

North Shore

Minnesota stretch of Lake Superior shoreline between Duluth and the Canadian border

Resort

Small family-owned motel and/or cabins often located on the lake and regularly visited by less-fortunate families who do not own a cabin

Turn to page 297 for more Minnesotisms.

Familiar Old Friends

Betty Crocker, the Jolly Green Giant, the Pillsbury Doughboy . . . Birthplace: Minnesota.

The Most Famous Minnesotan Who Never Was

As the popularity of General Mills' Gold Medal flour soared, women throughout America turned to the company with their baking questions. During the first decades of the 20th century, the company was barraged by thousands of letters each year from women asking for cooking advice. General Mills' management team decided that each letter should be answered and that all letters should bear a common signature to make the interaction between company and customer more personal. Rather than recruit a celebrity or hire someone for the job, the folks at General Mills cobbled together a fictitious name to represent them: "Betty" was a popular first name at the time; "Crocker" came from a recently retired General Mills executive (William G. Crocker). And so, in 1921, Betty Crocker was born.

The company held a contest among its female employees to pick Betty's signature. One of the secretaries won, and even though she remains anonymous, her signature still appears on all Betty Crocker products.

In 1924, General Mills put Betty on the radio. The *Betty*

Crocker Cooking School of the Air was the first in a long tradition of American cooking shows. It first aired on a local Minneapolis radio station and later on the NBC radio network. Thirteen different actresses working at radio stations around the country provided Betty's voice.

Hey, That's My Nose!

By 1936, fans were bursting with curiosity about what Betty looked like. Because she wasn't real, the General Mills advertising team couldn't just take a picture. Instead, the company hired Neysa McMein, a popular illustrator of the time, to give Betty Crocker a face. McMein studied and then combined facial features of all the women in the company's Home Service Department to create an official Betty Crocker portrait.

Over the years, Betty's portrait has evolved to keep up with changing trends and styles. From the somewhat stern older woman in the 1936 original, Betty's visage has changed seven times to reflect changing aesthetics; she has become younger and softer with each incarnation.

As different as they look, all Betty Crockers have certain traits in common because it wouldn't do to confuse the customers. All Bettys wear a red suit or dress with white at the neck—whether from a blouse, bow, ribbon, or string of pearls. Her look complete, Betty just needed some official recognition. In 1945, paying homage to her incomparable influence on American baking, *Fortune* magazine named Betty Crocker the second-most-famous woman in the United States. First was Eleanor Roosevelt, the then First Lady.

A Giant Success

In 1903, the Minnesota Valley Canning Company in Le Sueur began marketing canned vegetables. The company's first product, cream-style white corn, was immediately popular; 11,750 cases sold in the first year. Over the next two decades, the company added more products and, in 1925, introduced what became its signature product: an unusually large, sweet, and tender pea called "Green Giant."

He Towers Over All the Rest

The company hired advertising executives at the Leo Burnett agency in Chicago to come up with a campaign to promote the product, and the Green Giant, a symbol to represent the new pea, was born. The original giant was not the pleasant icon we know today. In his early days, he was "stooped, scowling, wore a scruffy bearskin and looked more like the Incredible Hulk than the happy gardener he is today." In the mid-1930s, however, the giant underwent a makeover because his countenance and demeanor were scaring the very children who were supposed to eat his products. His scowl was replaced by a smile, his posture improved, and he wore leafy clothes. The company's advertisers added the word "jolly" to his name and gave him his signature "Ho ho ho" utterance. They also posed him against the backdrop of a verdant (Minnesota) valley.

It's Not Just the Peas

The Jolly Green Giant brought his company so much success that, in 1950, the Minnesota Valley Canning Company became "Green Giant" and trademarked the name to represent all its products. Among the company's most popular offerings were frozen corn on the cob and jarred mushrooms (both introduced in 1969 and still sold today).

In 1979, Green Giant merged with the Pillsbury Company, another Minnesota success story. But that hasn't brought down its spokes-giant. In fact, he has become one of the most recognized advertising symbols in the world. Now, that's a jolly accomplishment for a giant who started out very unjolly indeed.

The Pillsbury Doughboy (Tee Hee)

It was 1965, and a group of creative types at the Leo Burnett advertising agency (the same place that conceived the Jolly Green Giant) were trying to come up with an ad campaign for refrigerated dough manufactured by Minneapolis's Pillsbury Company. In the meeting, copywriter Rudy Perz broke open a can. When the dough popped out of its tubular container, Perz got the idea for a character named "Poppin' Fresh."

Perz originally conceived of Poppin' Fresh as a two-dimensional character. But when he saw a film technique called "stop-action motion" used during the credits of the *Dinah Shore Show*, he realized he could turn Poppin' Fresh into a three-dimensional Doughboy. The process was slow and costly. To animate Poppin' Fresh took 24 separate images per second, and the original clay doll used in the commercials cost $16,000 to develop.

Dear Doughboy

Always wearing his chef's hat and neck scarf, the Doughboy

has, over the years, found himself in a variety of situations: He has appeared as a rock star, a ballet dancer, a skydiver, and a painter. He has also played many musical instruments, including a violin, guitar, accordion, and harmonica. But most of the commercials end the same way—a finger pokes him in his squishy stomach, and the Doughboy gives his characteristic giggle.

Poppin' Fresh's first voice was that of Paul Frees, the actor who also played the voice of Boris Badenov in the Rocky and Bullwinkle television cartoons. Jeff Bergman, who also did the voice of Charlie the Tuna, took over after Frees's death. Actor JoBe Cerny is the current Doughboy.

The Doughboy has become one of the most successful advertising icons in history. He receives hundreds of letters each year from his fans, and when Pillsbury issued a Doughboy doll in 1972, it was named "Toy of the Year" by *Playthings* magazine.

To read the General Mills story, turn to page 139.
To read the Pillsbury story, turn to page 223.

DID YOU KNOW?

Storms on Lake Superior can create waves that are more than 20 feet high.

Nine Things You Didn't Know About "Winnie"

*Although he's best known for his years as a New York Yankee,
power-hitter Dave "Winnie" Winfield was born in Saint Paul
and is one of Minnesota's favorite native sons.*

1. He could have been an Oriole.

In 1969, the Baltimore Orioles chose Winfield in the amateur
draft. He chose instead to go to the University of Minnesota on
a baseball scholarship. While in college, Winfield was a starting
pitcher before he suffered a shoulder injury. The setback did
have an upside, though; it forced him to focus on his hitting.
That change helped Winnie hit .385 and score eight home runs
and 33 RBIs during his senior college season. Along the way, he
also helped lead the Gophers to the semifinals of the College
World Series, where he was named MVP.

2. He was drafted in 1973 by four teams in three different sports.

Winfield's prowess on the diamond has been well documented,
but the six-foot-six sensation was also a phenomenal basketball
player who played power forward for the Gophers' hoops
squad. That versatility created some intriguing possibilities.
Following his university career, Winfield was drafted by

baseball's San Diego Padres, the NBA's Atlanta Hawks, the ABA's Utah Stars, and the NFL's Minnesota Vikings. What makes the Vikings selection all the more extraordinary is that Winfield never played a down of college football. The pick itself was something of a novelty for the Vikings, who chose Winfield with their final pick in the 17th round, hoping they could convince him to use his size and skilled hands on a football field rather than a baseball diamond.

3. He never played in the minors.
The Padres considered Winfield such a surefire prospect that he became one of the few players to jump directly from the amateur ranks to the major leagues. Despite his lack of time on "the farm," Winfield flourished and hit .277 during his rookie campaign.

4. He liked to play with pitchers' heads.
One of the most fearsome batters in the game, Winfield liked to psych out his opponents by swinging a sledgehammer in the on-deck circle.

5. He spent time in Canada's doghouse.
Winfield made headlines for all the wrong reasons on August 4, 1983, when he accidentally killed a seagull with a thrown ball during a game in Toronto. After the game, police escorted Winfield to the Ontario Provincial Police Station, where he was charged with cruelty to animals and forced to pay a $500 bond. The charges were eventually dropped.

6. His birthday has historical significance.

Mention October 3, 1951, to baseball fans, and they'll think of two things: Dave Winfield's birthday and the "shot heard 'round the world." Winfield was born the same day that New York Giants outfielder Bobby Thomson connected with a pennant-winning hit. Winfield had a similar moment himself in 1992, when his 11th inning, two-out double allowed the Toronto Blue Jays to win their first world championship. It was also the first World Series title won by a non–United States team.

7. He was Major League Baseball's oldest player during the 1995 season.

Winfield spent his final professional season in Cleveland as baseball's reigning old man. The 43-year-old appeared in 46 games and scored his last two home runs for the Indians.

8. He got George Steinbrenner booted out of baseball.

Winfield repeatedly knocked heads with Yankees owner George Steinbrenner during his nine years with the club. For the most part, Winnie could stand the public chiding, but when Steinbrenner refused to pay the Winfield Foundation the $300,000 guaranteed in Winfield's contract, the ballplayer decided to take the matter to court. Incensed, the Yankees boss tried to ruin Winfield's reputation by paying a gambler named Howie Spira $40,000 to uncover dirt on his star player. It didn't take long for Steinbrenner's scheme to become public, and Major League Baseball commissioner Fay Vincent suspended him from running the Yankees for two years beginning on July 20, 1990. In the end, neither Spira nor Steinbrenner was able to tarnish Winfield's reputation.

9. He was the first Hall of Famer to enter Cooperstown as a Padre.

One of baseball's traditions is that players entering the Hall of Fame get to choose which team's hat they wear on their official plaque. When it came time for Winfield to decide where his allegiances lay, the decision was an easy one. Despite spending his most productive years as a Yankee, Winnie decided to reward the franchise that gave him his start by entering Cooperstown as a Padre. The decision so angered George Steinbrenner that he tried (and failed) to have it reversed.

Career Stats:
- Winfield played for 22 seasons (1973–1995).
- He won seven Gold Gloves.
- He was a 12-time All Star.
- He batted .283, hit 465 home runs, and accumulated 3,110 hits.
- He played for six Major League teams: the San Diego Padres, New York Yankees, California Angels, Toronto Blue Jays, Minnesota Twins, and Cleveland Indians.

DID YOU KNOW?

Minnesota's smallest church is in the southwestern town of Luverne. The Blue Mound Wayside Chapel on Highway 75 seats four to six parishioners and a minister, though on busy Sundays, as many as eight people crowd inside.

In a Creative State

*You might be surprised at how many everyday
things were invented by Minnesotans.*

The Pop-Up Toaster

In the early 1900s, the electric toaster was not much more than
a wire cage next to a heating filament. The user had to flip the
bread and remove it when it was done, which led to a lot of
burned toast. In 1919, a Stillwater, Minnesota, factory worker
named Charles Strite figured out how to have the toast pop up
automatically. The Toastmaster, which incorporated his
designs, was first sold to the public in 1926.

Kitty Litter

For years, cat owners were faced with a messy problem: litter
boxes were filled with ash and sawdust that felines tracked
throughout the house. When a neighbor came to Saint Paul
native Edward Lowe with complaints about her kitty's dirty
dealings, Lowe suggested she use clay granules instead. She
took his suggestion and was so enthusiastic about the result
that, in 1947, Lowe packed 10 five-pound bags of clay granules, named the product "Kitty Litter," and, in an effort to
judge demand, told a local pet store to give it away. Soon, customers were clamoring for more and were willing to pay for it.

So Lowe sold the bags to pet stores out of the trunk of his car. Kitty Litter became a multimillion dollar empire that earned even more money when Lowe came out with the Tidy Cats brand of litter in 1964.

The Snowmobile

Although not technically the first to build a snowmobile (a Ford dealer actually takes that title after mounting a Model T onto skis and calling it a "snowmobile"), a Roseau, Minnesota, farm equipment company called Polaris Industries was the first to sell a snowmobile to the public. The first Polaris model arrived in January 1956. It was a bulky machine that had a grain elevator conveyor belt for a track and parts of a Chevy's bumper for skis and sold for $465. Over the next decade, the company tried, failed, and tried again to create a snowmobile design that was reliable and easy to use. On the brink of bankruptcy, designers Alan and Edgar Heteen and David Johnson finally turned things around in the mid-1960s when they invented and sold the popular Mustang and Colt model snowmobiles. Polaris has been one of America's top snowmobile producers ever since.

The NordicTrack

Minnesotan Ed Pauls loved to cross-country ski, but he wasn't fond of training during wet, cold weather. So he decided to bring the training indoors. In 1975, he created several homemade stationary-skiing machines in his garage. He tried selling them, but no one was interested except the U.S. ski team, to whom he donated several models. However, when the exercise industry took off in the United States in the 1980s, Pauls's indoor skiing machine became a hit because it allowed users to get a total body workout without ever leaving their living rooms. Pauls originally called the machine the NordicJock, but later changed the name to NordicTrack when women complained the original name was sexist. By 1986, demand for NordicTrack machines exceeded what Pauls could create in his garage-turned-manufacturing-plant, so he sold the company and patent for $24 million.

Rollerblades

Sometimes it's a reinvention that takes the world by storm. In-line skates date back as far as the 18th century, but it wasn't until a pair of 20th century Minnesota brothers came along that the skates' popularity exploded. The year was 1980, and Scott and Brennan Olson, 19 and 20 years old respectively, were rummaging through a used sporting goods store in Minneapolis. They found an old pair of in-line roller skates, and they thought the design would make a great off-season training tool for hockey players. After several weeks of tinkering in their parents' basement, the Olson brothers perfected a new design, started a company, and came up with a name for the new skate: the Rollerblade. The brothers sold their company early on, but maintained royalty rights. So when in-line skating took off during the 1990s, they made millions.

The Small Town with a Big Reputation

Thanks to two local businesses, the name Red Wing
has come to represent old-fashioned quality.

For a small town (fewer than 17,000 residents), Red Wing, Minnesota, has built a mighty big reputation. Located in the southeast part of the state on the banks of the Mississippi River and near the Wisconsin border, Red Wing is internationally known for two basic and well-crafted products: stoneware and shoes.

Going to Pot

The Red Wing Stoneware Company has a reputation for producing prized stoneware, though it didn't start out prized; it started out practical. The pottery became popular because it was durable, everyday kitchenware and indispensable for storing food. Before refrigeration, root cellars and crocks (with water- and rodent-proof lids) were the best ways to safeguard food and ensure that it didn't spoil.

Buried Treasure

Clay is the fundamental ingredient in stoneware. Pure clay is especially good because it can withstand very high temperatures during the firing process. The pure clay deposit found just outside Red Wing is one of the largest in the United States. This rich resource would ultimately prove vital to Minnesota's stoneware industry, and it was only a matter of time before someone took advantage.

In 1877, a group of investors formed the Red Wing Stoneware Company. Production began in January 1878, and by August, the company already had a reputation for creating useful and beautiful products. Crocks, churns, dinnerware, and other utilitarian pieces were the most popular products, though flowerpots and vases also sometimes made their way out of the kilns.

Eventually, other stoneware companies emerged, and competition was fierce. So at the turn of the 20th century, the Red Wing Stoneware Company and other local stoneware manufacturers (the Minnesota Stoneware Company, the North Star Stoneware Company, and the Red Wing Stoneware and Sewer Pipe Company) merged to form the Red Wing Union Stoneware Company. Over the next 100 years, the company survived a disastrous kiln fire and a workers' strike. It also closed, reopened, and changed hands (and names) several times. Today, the Red Wing Stoneware Company produces both practical and novelty products.

That's a Crock!

The older Red Wing crocks have become collector's items. Every year, folks gather at the Red Wing Collector's Society convention (in Red Wing, of course), where they buy, sell, and trade crocks and other stoneware pieces.

Prices are high; a crock that originally sold for a nominal amount might fetch more than $400 today. Then there are the rare pieces, like the 1890s 20-gallon, sand-colored stoneware crock that collector Lyle Berman bought in 2002 for $37,000. Red Wing stoneware collectors generally agree that the original pottery is worth its high price because it is durable, beautiful, and, says one collector, "it gets in your blood."

Step on It!

If stoneware was Red Wing's contribution to the early 20th century housewife, shoes were its gift to the blue-collar worker. The Red Wing Shoe Company sold its first pair of boots in 1905, and since then, the company has churned out boots for miners, steelworkers, soldiers, and even celebrities.

Businessman Charles H. Beckman founded the Red Wing Shoe Company. Boot making wasn't new to him, however. Beckman spent several years working for another popular local shoemaker, the Foot-Sterling Shoe Factory, before he decided to break out on his own in 1905.

Beckman's company was small but efficient. His workers could make more than 100 pairs of boots per day. The boots were more durable than comparable brands and more comfortable, crafted from quality leather treated at local tanneries. They were also affordable. The first pair of Red Wing boots cost only $1.75.

Regional consumers, especially miners and construction workers, quickly became enamored with Red Wing boots. But a contract with the U.S. Army introduced the product to a large audience. In 1915, the Red Wing Shoe Company worked to meet the Army's growing demand for shoes. Production of Red

Wing boots skyrocketed to 200,000 pairs annually as World War I soldiers wore their Red Wings into battle. When the war ended, the soldiers brought their love of the shoes home with them. Sales boomed during the 1920s and then again during World War II, when the Red Wing Shoe Company manufactured 239 different sizes of boots for U.S. soldiers.

Today, the Red Wing Shoe Company continues to make shoes in the small Minnesota town where it all began. The company has also maintained its reputation for quality and comfort and has expanded its brand to create dressy work shoes as well as boots. Construction workers, stockbrokers, and others still clamor for Red Wing shoes. Even a celebrity or two have been known to wear them: former president George Bush and musician Eric Clapton are rumored to be fans.

Fun Facts:

- In celebration of its centennial, the Red Wing Shoe Company crafted a gigantic boot. It took 4,000 hours of labor volunteered by more than 60 employees (both current and retired) to design, engineer, and build the size $638\frac{1}{2}$ D classic style 877 boot.

- During the 1960s, artists Norman Rockwell and Les Kuba created artwork for the Red Wing Shoe Company's catalogs and ads.

- Red Wing's founding fathers borrowed the town's name from Dakota tribal leaders who wore scarlet-dyed swans' wings. Both the Red Wing Shoe Company and the Red Wing Stoneware Company have, in turn, honored the town and its heritage with their own bright red wing logos.

Greyhound by the Numbers

Say the name "Greyhound," and you're sure to think of the largest transcontinental bus service in North America.

In 1914, Minnesotan Carl Wickman noticed that miners traveling from Hibbing to nearby Alice needed transportation. He quickly founded a bus company to provide it. From these humble beginnings, Greyhound Lines (so named because greyhounds are the fastest canine breed) evolved into the monster passenger transport enterprise it is today.

4

Names the company has used since its inception (Mesaba Transportation Company, Motor Transit Corporation, Northland Transportation Company, and Greyhound)

7.2

Average age of a Greyhound bus in 2005

13

Freedom Riders who, in 1961, rode a Greyhound bus into the Deep South to protest racial segregation

15 cents

Amount Wickman charged his first passengers per ride

$45

Average cost of a current Greyhound ticket

1915

Year Carl Wickman joined forces with Ralph Bogan, who ran a transit service in Duluth. The two merged their companies and called the new organization the Mesaba Transportation Company.

1929

Year the company took the name Greyhound Lines

1930

Year Greyhound moved its corporate headquarters from Duluth to Chicago; the company moved two more times: to Phoenix in 1971 and to Dallas in 1987.

2,500

Drivers currently employed by Greyhound

16,000

Scheduled daily departures across North America

22 million

Passengers carried by Greyhound buses each year

7.1 billion

Passenger miles traveled by Greyhound buses in 2005

Soaked Till Scrumptious!

No one knows for certain why Viking culture died out, but some have suggested that lutefisk had something to do with it.

It is sometimes said that the Scandinavian countries include Norway, Sweden, Denmark, and Minnesota. It is no wonder, then, that Scandinavian culinary specialties bring tears of nostalgia to some Minnesotans' eyes. And few dishes evoke such emotion more than lutefisk . . . although it could be argued that the tears actually form at the mere thought of eating this pungent "delicacy."

Lutefisk is traditionally eaten at Christmas and sometimes during other celebrations. But few people, even among its most die-hard devotees, eat the dish more than once a year, if then.

Tell Me No Lye

You've heard of lye. It's the stuff you pour down your drain when it's clogged. Well, lutefisk is basically dried cod that has been soaked in lye for several days, at which point it becomes highly poisonous.

Before the fish is edible, it must be soaked in cold water (changed daily) for several days. You may then proceed with your favorite recipe; this usually entails boiling the fish in salted water until it acquires a characteristic (and some might say scrumptious) gelatinous texture. Scandinavians swear by the stuff, and so do many Minnesotans of Nordic heritage.

How It Began

The origins of lutefisk are shrouded in mystery. We do know that, in the days before refrigeration, drying fish was one of the most common methods of preserving it. One common legend claims that a dried cod fell into a bowl of cleaning solution containing lye. Waste not, want not, the frugal Nordic housewife believed. So she rinsed off the fish and served the tainted morsel to her family, who not only lived, but developed a taste for it.

An alternative, more plausible, theory is that a fish-drying wooden rack caught fire, and the fish fell into the ashes. Several rainy days followed (this legend takes place in Norway, after all). Since wood ash and water combine to form lye, there you have it: lutefisk.

Whatever the actual origin of the delicacy, nowadays there is no longer a need to go through the arduous soaking process. Frozen and adequately soaked lutefisk is readily available at selected grocery stores.

So eat up like a good little Viking. And don't let the occasional fish bone deter you from enjoying this rubbery, jellied treat.

Mystery Science Theater 3000

Hey! Who are those guys at the bottom of the screen, and
why don't they shut up so I can watch the movie?

In 1988, KTMA, a public access cable channel in Minneapolis, needed to fill up a two-hour time slot in its Sunday evening lineup. The station's executives turned to Jim Mallon, their production manager, who called on his friends Joel Hodgson, Trace Beaulieu, and Kevin Murphy. After some brainstorming and thought, Joel suggested airing a terrible film while he and two puppets mocked it from the front row of a theater. Silly as the premise sounded, KTMA was the last-rated station in its market; expectations were not high. So the four cobbled together a few crude puppets, watched half an hour of a movie called *The Green Slime,* and ad-libbed comments. The show, called *Mystery Science Theater 3000,* debuted on Thanksgiving Day, 1988.

Meet MST3K

The original premise of the show (called *MST3K* by fans) was that Joel Robinson (played by Joel Hodgson), a janitor at a scientific center called the Gizmonic Institute, was sent into space by his mad scientist bosses. Joel hangs out on a spaceship called the *Satellite of Love*, where the Mads (as the scientists are known) force him to watch bad films while they monitor his brain.

For company, Joel built himself robot companions called 'bots. While the film plays, the silhouettes of Joel and the 'bots appear in the bottom right-hand corner of the screen. Crow T. Robot, who looks like a deranged reindeer with half a bowling pin for a beak and the front of a hockey mask rising like antlers from the back of his head, was named for a friend of a childhood acquaintance of Hodgson's. In a KTMA-era host segment, the character of Joel told Crow his name stood for "Cybernetic Remotely Operated Woman," even though Crow was operated and voiced by the male Trace Beaulieu. In case you're curious, the middle initial *T* stands for "the."

The other movie-mocker, Tom Servo, whose head is an empty gumball machine, was named for a "Servotron" vending machine. Also present on the *Satellite of Love* were Cambot the camera and Gypsy, a vaguely Miss Piggy–like conglomeration of Tupperware and tubing.

Over the years, the show's premise changed somewhat, but the movie watching stayed the same. *MST3K* lampooned the classics of bad film (Ed Wood, Bela Lugosi, *Godzilla*), along with TV movies, a Lassie film, and even an episode of *Gumby*. Most of the heckled movies, though, were the type of plotless, badly acted dreck that few people have ever heard of. Some of the classic episodes featured *Santa Claus Conquers the Martians, Viking Women vs. the Sea Serpent, Teenagers from Outer Space, Monster A Go-Go,* and *Eegah!* The first season screened only sci-fi and horror films, but over the years, *MST3K* aired westerns, dramas, and teen angst flicks with equal impunity. When the movies ran short, the crew filled up the time with short films procured from New York film historian Rick Prelinger. These were mostly educational films on subjects like posture or car salesmen that readily lent themselves to ridicule.

Calling Comedy Central

MST3K ran on KTMA from November 1988 through May 1989. During that period, the station received a lot of mail about the show. Some of the letters contained enthusiastic praise, but most voiced confusion as to what the strange characters were doing. In fact, several letters complained about the guys talking through the movie; how was one to follow the story if the characters talked through it?

Nevertheless, Mallon thought the show was special, and he headed to New York to pitch it to two national cable comedy channels: *HA!* and the fledgling Comedy Channel, now known as Comedy Central. *HA!* decided to pass, but the Comedy Channel bought 13 episodes of *MST3K*. Today, Mallon and company joke that they'd like to believe the Comedy Channel execs saw the genius of *MST3K*, but more likely the station managers were trying to fill up their schedules, and the low-cost two-hour program fit the bill. No matter. Joel and the 'bots were going national.

Simply the Best

The first nationally televised *MST3K* episode, "The Crawling Eye," aired on the Comedy Channel in November 1989. With the new station came slight changes in the show's premise (a new setting called Deep 13 was introduced; the Gizmonic Institute was slowly phased out) and new characters (Magic Voice, for instance), but the move proved a good one. *MST3K* steadily picked up devoted fans (called MSTies), and when the Comedy Channel almost canceled the show, the fans saved it by deluging the studio with pleas to keep the movies coming. MSTies even created parody videos using the format of the show, the most famous of which heckles *Star Trek V.*

The show tried to reward these loyal fans. Its creators ran a fan club (carried over from their old KTMA days) to keep viewers abreast of the news from the *Satellite of Love.* And from 1991 to 1995, Comedy Central made Thanksgiving the high holiday of MSTies by airing an annual "Turkey Day" marathon—30 hours of heckling from Best Brains Inc., the company Mallon and his team founded to produce the show.

The Great Flame War of '93

Joel Hodgson left the show halfway through season five. He was frustrated by the grind of producing and starring in a weekly show. He wanted to play a larger role behind the scenes and to develop new projects.

Longtime head writer Mike Nelson was the logical choice to replace Hodgson as host. Some MSTies were happy with Nelson and considered him a fresh addition to the show. Others, Hodgson purists, were outraged. Thus began the "Great Mike-versus-Joel Flame War of 1993."

MST3K was one of the first shows to benefit from the popularity of the Internet, and it gained a huge online fan following in the early 1990s. With the change in hosts, online discussion boards were flooded with posts debating the comparative merits of Joel and Mike. Polite discourse degenerated into name-calling, and soon the online MSTies were tearing out one another's cybernetic throats. Internet boards abounded with vitriolic posts called "flames" in Internet slang. Later, Joel Hodgson admitted to provoking fans by posting on discussion boards under a pseudonym. As is the case with most Internet outrage, the debate settled down after awhile, but be forewarned: even now, discussion of this topic among MSTies is strictly verboten.

The End

Despite the strife among fans, *MST3K* continued to thrive in the ratings under Mike Nelson. Comedy Central kept it on the air through its seventh season. After that station canceled the show, the SciFi Channel picked it up and produced three more seasons. Best Brains even made an *MST3K* movie, released to limited engagement on April 19, 1996.

The final episode of *MST3K* aired on August 8, 1999. In it, Mike and the 'bots returned to Earth after their 10-year-long adventure in space. The last host segment showed them settling into freedom: They sat on a couch and watched an old movie called *The Crawling Eye*. As the show came to an end, Crow realized the movie seemed awfully familiar.

Intellectual Property, Feh

MST3K may be one of the oddest shows ever to air. Nevertheless, it was nominated for eight CableACE awards and two Emmys for writing during its run. It even won a Peabody

Award. But you won't be seeing it returning in syndication any time soon. Since every episode featured a different movie, Best Brains had to secure the rights to each film individually. Now that those original agreements have expired, potential distributors have had a hard time securing the rights again. In fact, Sandy Frank, one of the producers of many a mocked film, has reportedly said it will be a cold day in hell before he ever lets *MST3K* get its hands on his films again. All Joel and the guys did was bring Frank's movies to a national TV audience. What's he so sore about?

DID YOU KNOW?

In Sanborn, a few miles up the Laura Ingalls Wilder Highway (U.S. highway 14) from Walnut Grove, is a replica of a 19th century sod house. It belongs to Stan McCone, who built it to recreate his great grandparents' South Dakota homestead. McCone began work on the replica in the late 1980s and finished it a few years later. The house is now a bed-and-breakfast; it's heated by a wood stove, lit by oil lamps, and includes a sod outhouse instead of a bathroom so that visitors can get a taste of what life on the Minnesota prairie was like more than 100 years ago.

The "Body" Speaks

*Former Minnesota governor and professional wrestler Jesse
"the Body" Ventura has had a lot to say over the years.*

The Good . . .

"A third-party candidate is never treated equally. They look at
you as a novelty, as cannon fodder. 'This is entertaining,' they
think, 'but we'll go back to the Democrats and Republicans,
because only they can run our government.' Which is baloney."

"I didn't need this job. I ran for governor to find out if the
American dream still exists in anyone's heart other than mine.
I'm living proof that the myths aren't true. The candidate with
the most money isn't always the one who wins."

"No law will make a citizen a patriot."

The Bad . . .

"I think, in 2008, we need a pro wrestler in the White House."

"I asked [the Dalai Lama] the most important question that I
think you could ask—if he had ever seen *Caddyshack*."

"Wrestling is ballet with violence."

"If I could be reincarnated as a fabric, I would come back as a 38 double-D bra."

"I'm kind of like Che Guevara. I lead the revolution, but at some point, I turn it over to someone else."

And the Ugly . . .

"If you were to come to Minnesota, I could have you locked up like that. That's power."

"If you are smart enough to go to college, you are smart enough to figure out a way to pay for it."

"If you're a feeble, weak-minded person to begin with, I don't have time for you."

DID YOU KNOW?

Pipestone, or catlinite, is a soft red rock that many Native American tribes use to make ceremonial smoking pipes. For more than 11,000 years, tribes mined pipestone from quarries located in southwestern Minnesota and South Dakota. These quarries were sacred to the tribes, and all agreed to share them. No wars were ever fought there, so Europeans dubbed the pipes made from that stone "peace pipes." Today, the area is part of the Pipestone National Monument, and tribes still gather rock from its quarries to make their pipes.

If Cargill Were a Country

In 1868, W. W. Cargill moved his food and products business to Minnesota, riding a post–Civil War economic boom. In the century that followed, his enterprise turned into an industrial empire whose scale and success were equal to that of most nations. Just how would Cargill measure up if it were its own country?

It would have 61 embassies.

Cargill operates in 61 countries and has more than 1,000 actual locations. In addition to its U.S. workforce, the company employs people in three international divisions: Europe/Africa, Latin America, and Asia/Pacific. That totals more than 100,000 employees worldwide.

It would have a GDP higher than Kuwait, Syria, or Luxembourg.

In 2005, Cargill had sales and other revenues of more than $71 billion. That means the company's revenue from that year could have bought 40,000 luxury yachts, 116,695 brand new Ferrari F430s, and Bill Gates (based on average 2005 Microsoft stock prices), and there would still be enough leftover to buy $100,000 worth of Cartier jewelry. That's also enough cash to write every living person in Minnesota a check for almost $15,000. And all that after donating $20 million annually to nonprofit organizations worldwide.

It would handle more cotton than Turkmenistan.

Cargill's cotton division merchandises 4 million bales of cotton annually. That's enough to make 860 million pairs of blue jeans, 5 billion pillowcases, or 2 billion fluffy bath towels.

It would provide its own power.

Forget OPEC. Cargill has helped to develop ways of producing power from corn (ethanol) and continues to investigate the use of other biofuels that would result in less dependence on oil. It runs and builds ethanol plants around the world. Cargill is also one of North America's largest shippers of both natural gas and power; the company trades in electricity, natural gas, and other resources.

It would rule by hereditary monarchy.

Unlike many other corporations with this financial prowess, Cargill is a privately owned company. From the company's founding in the mid-1800s until today, Cargill has been owned by the Cargill family. In fact, 85 percent of the company is still owned by descendants of the company's founders.

It would have impeccable credit.

Cargill has a 5A1 credit score, the highest measure of financial strength (5A companies have more than $50,000,000 in sales) paired with the best possible record for paying its bills (1 = super good credit).

It would be a leader in food production.

Already, Cargill mines 10 percent of the world's salt, produces almost 20 percent of the world's turkey products and 22 percent of America's beef products, ships 31 percent of America's soybeans, and buys more of China's corn products than anyone else. The company is also in the business of making or supporting the production of chocolate, sugar, sugar substitutes, grits, malt, corn oil, soy protein, eggs, French toast, oxtails, sunflower oil, grains, canola oil, starch, and more.

It would handle 25 times more sugar than Barbados.

Cargill trades and ships more than 9 million metric tons of sugar every year. That's enough sugar to sweeten 826,500,000 Venti-sized Starbucks Coconut Crème Frappuccinos.

It would have its own mini–Wall Street.

Cargill's Financial and Risk Management division does everything from purchasing real estate to devising investment strategies to investing venture capital into early-stage technology companies. The Cargill Value Investment group has more than 70 investment professionals on staff and operates out of a mansion on Lake Minnetonka.

DID YOU KNOW?

Gangster Lester Gillis, better known as Baby Face Nelson, held up the First National Bank in Brainerd, Minnesota, on October 27, 1933, and escaped with $32,000. A year later, following the death of John Dillinger, Nelson became the FBI's Public Enemy Number One.

Minnesotisms: Food

*Still talking like a native, we hope. Here's the last
installment in the "speaking Minnesotan" series.*

Minnesotans like to eat. These are things you'll need to know
about Minnesota's meals and menus.

Lutefisk
Pronounced: *LU-ta-fisk*
Dried codfish, soaked in lye until the consistency of Jell-O.
Served with melted butter or white sauce. Minnesotans know
this is a delicacy, and since they're so nice, they'll be happy to
share.

Lefse
Pronounced: *Lef-SAH*
Potato-and-flour flatbread

Jell-O Salad
Any of a number of concoctions made by combining Jell-O
with fruits, vegetables, whipped cream, sour cream, cottage
cheese, and/or marshmallows. The common variety typically
contains lime-green Jell-O, crushed pineapple, and cottage
cheese.

Bars

A dessert most often baked in a large pan and cut into squares. Necessary ingredients include chocolate chips, oatmeal, butter, and eggs.

Dinner

Lunch (to people outside Minnesota)

Supper

Dinner (to people outside Minnesota)

A Little Lunch

An afternoon snack, most often including coffee and cookies or bars

DID YOU KNOW?

In 1887, Saint Paul grocer P. J. Towle decided he wanted to create a syrup that had the taste of maple but the lower cost of sugar syrup. Towle wanted to name his new product after Abraham Lincoln, one of the people Towle most admired. But there were already so many products named for the former president that Towle decided instead to call his syrup Log Cabin Syrup after the president's birthplace.

Gone Fishin'

How well do you know your Minnesota fish? Take our quiz to find out.

1. The most sought-after fish for Minnesota anglers is a
   A. Northern pike
   B. Salmon
   C. Walleye

2. The easiest fish to catch (because it's aggressive and so willing to bite a lure or bait) is a
   A. Northern pike
   B. Walleye
   C. Sunfish

3. One good way to tell a muskie from a northern pike is to
A. Weigh them; a muskie will weigh about half as much as a pike.
B. Count the pores on each side of the underside of the fish's jaw (a muskie has six or more on each side; a northern pike has five or fewer).
C. Look at their tails; a northern pike has pointy tail fins, whereas a muskie has rounded tail fins.

4. The walleye is so named because

A. It has opaque, silvery, "walleyed" eyes.

B. Norse legends tell of a half-man/half-fish whose love for (and distrust of) a local maiden was so strong that he rose out of Lake Mjosa and became the "eyes on the wall" of her home to make sure she remained true to him.

C. A North Country kid named Walley was the first to catch one in Minnesota waters.

5. A sauger looks a lot like which other type of fish?

    A. Trout

    B. Salmon

    C. Walleye

6. Oh, crappie! Which Minnesota county holds the record for the largest black crappie catch (21 inches long and weighing 5 pounds)?

    A. Faribault

    B. Dakota

    C. Ramsey

For answers, turn to page 309.

DID YOU KNOW?

International Falls, Minnesota, inspired the fictional town of Frostbite Falls, home of cartoon characters Rocky and Bullwinkle.

The Gang's Last Stand

When the James-Younger gang rode into Northfield, Minnesota, on September 7, 1876, their plan was to rob a bank. The townspeople, however, had other ideas, and the band of burgling brothers was never the same.

When the Civil War ended in 1865, pro-Confederate guerrilla fighters Jesse and Frank James were in a bind: they couldn't surrender for fear of being shot by the conquering Union army, and they certainly didn't want to ally themselves with their former enemies. Figuring there was safety in numbers, the brothers teamed up with another group of siblings that had sided with the South during the war: the Youngers, specifically Cole, Bob, and Jim. The James and Younger brothers (and a few other outlaws) formed the James-Younger gang, a group of criminals determined to get back at the Northern victors. For the next 10 years, the James-Younger gang went on a violent crime spree throughout the reunified United States. They robbed banks, stores, stagecoaches, and individuals and even committed murder. In 1873, they pulled off the first train robbery, killing the engineer and stealing $3,000 from passengers. These activities earned them a reputation in 19th century America, and members of the James-Younger gang soon became among the most wanted and notorious criminals of their time.

In 1876, Bill Stiles, a James-Younger gang member from Minnesota, suggested that his home state would be an easy target for a bank robbery. Stiles believed the banks there were full of money and that the locals (mostly farmers) would be poor shots and unable to defend themselves. The gang posed as railroad surveyors and cased various Minnesota cities, including Red Wing, Saint Paul, and Mankato, before deciding on the First National Bank of Northfield. Northfield seemed a good choice. The bank was rumored to hold a lot of Union money, and the former Confederates were always looking for ways to get back at their old enemies. Given the relatively small size of the town and the experience of the gang, the job should have been easy.

Not in Our Town!

On the afternoon of September 7, 1876, eight gang members rode into Northfield wearing long coats that concealed their weapons. Frank James, Bob Younger, and Charlie Pitts entered the bank around two o'clock in the afternoon. Cole Younger and Clell Miller stood guard at the front door, while Jesse James, Jim Younger, and Bill Stiles protected the planned escape route.

Inside the bank, one of the robbers (possibly Frank James, though no one is certain) ordered cashier Joseph Lee Heywood to open the safe. Heywood refused. Things heated up when merchant J. S. Allen walked by the bank and noticed the commotion. He tried to get past Miller at the front door but couldn't; Miller shoved him away. Allen then ran off screaming that the bank was being robbed. In response, Miller and Cole Younger began shooting at him.

The unexpected gunfire startled the robbers and hostages inside the bank. Mayhem broke out. During the commotion, bank clerk A. E. Bunker made a mad dash out the back door, but not before taking a bullet in his shoulder. Frank James shot and killed Heywood, who went down still refusing to open the safe.

Meanwhile, the citizens of Northfield had armed themselves and taken up strategic positions around the town. They barraged the outlaws with bullets. Clell Miller and Bill Stiles fell dead in the street. Frank James was shot in the leg; Jesse rode by on a horse, grabbed his brother's arm, and pulled him along. The Younger brothers and Pitts also took bullets. Local resident Nicolas Gustafson was caught in the crossfire and died four days later of his wounds.

Living on the Lam

The outlaws headed for the woods to regroup. For the next week, the gang members sneaked through several tiny Minnesota towns, but they were lost and unable to find their way out of the area without Bill Stiles, who had known that part of the state well. They grew increasingly tired and hungry. Their injuries slowed them down, and their exhausted horses had to be abandoned. All the while, posses of townspeople and lawmen followed close behind. Finally, the James-Younger boys decided to split up. The James brothers stole two horses from a local farm and headed for Dakota Territory, while Charlie Pitts and the badly injured Younger brothers went west, eventually hiding near Madelia, Minnesota.

Time was running out for the Youngers and Pitts. The posses were hot on the criminals' trail, and just outside Madelia, only 50 miles from Northfield, a search party met up with the escapees. Pitts was killed in the ensuing gun battle, but the Youngers surrendered.

The Northfield raid proved to be the end of the James-Younger gang. The Youngers were each arrested and tried on four counts, including murder, attempted murder, and robbery. To avoid execution, the brothers pleaded guilty to the crimes (at the time, Minnesota law would not allow a death sentence for people who pleaded guilty). All three were sentenced to life in prison.

But the James brothers got away. After kidnapping a doctor to treat their wounds (and then releasing him), Jesse and Frank traveled to their home state of Missouri, where they formed a new gang and continued their lives as criminals. Lawmen all over the Midwest were still looking for them, however, and the governor of Missouri offered a $10,000 reward for their capture. In 1881, Bob Ford, one of the new James gang members, shot and killed Jesse to collect the reward. Frank turned himself in soon after and was tried but acquitted for his crimes.

Today, memory of the Northfield raid lives on in Minnesota. The First National Bank of Northfield has been restored as a museum, and each year the town's citizens celebrate the day their ancestors defeated the James-Younger gang's attempt to rob their bank. Held annually in September, the Defeat of Jesse James Days Festival includes a reenactment of the bank raid, a parade, and a graveside memorial service at the burial sites of Joseph Lee Heywood and Nicolas Gustafson.

How Much, You Say?

Just in case you were wondering, the outlaws didn't leave Northfield empty-handed. It wasn't quite the haul they'd hoped for, but the James-Younger gang did get away with $26.70. One of the boys grabbed the cash off the bank's counter as they fled the botched robbery.

DID YOU KNOW?

Many movies have been made about the gang's attempt to rob the First National Bank of Northfield. Two of the most well known are 1972's *The Great Northfield Minnesota Raid,* starring Cliff Robertson and Robert Duvall, and 1980's *The Long Riders.* The latter starred four sets of real-life brothers as members of the gang: David, Keith, and Robert Carradine play the Youngers; James and Stacy Keach portray Jesse and Frank James; Dennis and Randy Quaid play Ed and Clell Miller; and Christopher and Nicholas Guest portray Charlie and Bob Ford.

Answers

The Lake Effect, page 42

1. A. Lake Saganaga is 240 feet deep.

2. B. Mower, Olmsted, Pipestone, and Rock

3. A. Brownie Lake in Minneapolis comprises only 12 acres and is 47 feet deep.

    4. C. Lake Vermilion has 1,200 miles of shoreline and is the fifth largest lake in Minnesota.

5. B. Red Lake (Upper and Lower) is comprised of 288,800 acres.

6. A. Minnesota's 90,000 miles of shoreline is more than Florida, California, and Hawaii combined.

7. C. There are 201 lakes called Mud Lake. The nine next most common lake names are
    Rice Lake
    Bass Lake
    Round Lake
    Horseshoe Lake
    Twin Lake
    Island Lake
    Johnson Lake
    Spring Lake

8. B. Approximately 5 percent of the state is covered with water.

Let's Get Down to Business, page 50

1. B. Four other states have official muffins: Massachusetts (corn muffin), New York (apple muffin), Hawaii (coconut muffin), and Washington (blueberry muffin).
2. C. Loons are large water birds with wingspans that can reach five feet. They are black and white, have red eyes, and are known for their distinctive wails and yodels.
3. A. Five other states have voted the monarch as their state butterfly: Alabama, Idaho, Illinois, Texas, and West Virginia.
4. C. Walleyes live primarily in the large, clear, cool lakes of northern Minnesota because they are sensitive to light. During the day, they spend their time in deep, dark lakes, but they do move to shallow water at night.
5. A. Minnesota produces 6 percent of the milk in the United States, making it fifth among the states in dairy production.
6. A. The plant is also slow to mature. It can take up to 16 years to produce its first flowers.
7. B. There are several types of morel mushrooms, some poisonous and some edible. The edible ones have a reputation for being among the tastiest 'shrooms around.
8. A. Wild rice and common rice are two completely different plants. Wild rice is an aquatic grass that belongs to the *Zizania aquatica* species, and common rice is a cereal grain that belongs to the *Oryza sativa* species.
9. B. In 1945, the University of Minnesota Alumni Association released the song's music and words so that the Minnesota legislature could adopt "Hail! Minnesota" as the state song, but the organization still holds the copyright.
10. C. Red pines can live to be 400 years old!

"Trivial" Minnesota, page 68

Land of How Many Lakes?, page 162

The hidden message: Minnesota actually has more than ten thousand lakes!

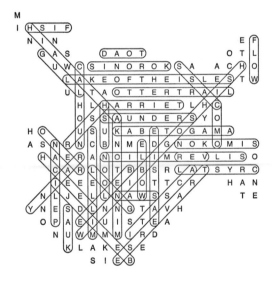

Wait! Where Am I?, page 188

1. B   2. C   3. D   4. A   5. A

Marquee Minnesota, page 204

Famous Minnesotans, page 250

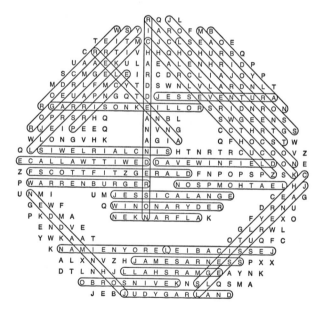

Gone Fishin', page 299

1. C   2. A   3. B   4. A   5. C   6. B

Be sure to check out more hot titles from

Available at bookstores, warehouse clubs, and in great bathrooms everywhere. Or visit www.bathroomreader.com.

Bathroom Readers' Press • P.O. Box 1117 • Ashland, OR 97520
Phone: 541–488–4642 • Fax: 541–482–6159